For the "Friend of American Writers"
with love -

Mummy

Out of the Woods

By Esther Kellner

OUT OF THE WOODS

THE BACKGROUND OF THE OLD TESTAMENT

THE BRIDE OF PILATE

MARY OF NAZARETH

THE PROMISE

Out of the Woods

by Esther Kellner

Doubleday & Company, Inc.
Garden City, New York
1964

Library of Congress Catalog Card Number 64–19294

Printed in the United States of America
First Edition

To Carl and Marjorie Nichols

Grateful Acknowledgments

to:

Dr. Richard W. Siebert (American Veterinary Medical Association, American Animal Hospital Association) . . . the skilled veterinarian who regularly cared for our little squirrels.

Gertrude Ward (naturalist, professor of biology, assistant director of the Joseph Moore Museum, Richmond, Indiana) . . . who read this script and furnished many valuable criticisms and suggestions.

Dr. Ralph E. Smith (American Veterinary Medical Association) . . . the resourceful general practitioner who saved Mimi's life when she had pneumonia.

Louis E. Ripberger (ornithologist, Wayne County chapter of the National Audubon Society) . . . whose knowledge and advice have helped us many times.

Dr. Bob Stevenson (American Veterinary Medical Association, public-relations director of the Ohio Veterinary Medical Association, staff veterinarian of the Dayton Museum of Natural History) . . . who has given us generously of his counsel, time, and skill.

Karl H. Maslowski (naturalist, natural-history columnist, photographer, lecturer, producer of wildlife and conservation films, trustee of the Cincinnati Museum of Natural History) . . . who has been of immeasurable assistance to us.

Anthony E. Hoover, M.S.N.L.S. (reference librarian, Morrison-Reeves Library, Richmond, Indiana) . . . who has given much time and interest to verifying certain items from the author's collection of animal, plant, and weather folklore.

Esther Kellner

Out of the Woods

I Sometimes I wake in the darkness just before dawn thinking I heard the old hunter call my name. I see the first redness of morning, feel the touch of the dawn wind, the sweet coolness of the woods, but it is another morning, another wind, the sweet coolness of a woods far away. And I did not hear him call me. His voice has been stilled for many years, and the grass blows over his grave.

"Old Bill" he was called, in affection, in respect, and sometimes in resignation. I never really knew how old he was, for he was as ageless as a character in a book, and he belonged in a book . . . the story of Jim Bridger or Tecumseh or Daniel Boone, of Indian fighters and trail blazers and pioneer scouts. It is not unusual to meet a man like Bill in fiction, but I never knew anyone else like him in real life, for he belonged to another era. He had been born a hundred years too late, and in the world to which he came he was a lonely misfit.

I suppose he was nearing seventy when I first knew him, though he looked much younger. He was a lean, muscular old man with a shock of white hair which he trimmed raggedly with the scissors whenever it grew long enough to annoy him. His face was leathery and lined and tanned. He had huge hands and feet and a peculiarly cautious gait which came from many years of following game in the silent Indian fashion. His movements often appeared awkward and clumsy, yet when he wished he could pass through a thicket in August without snapping a twig or breaking a branch.

In winter he wore thick cowhide shoes with long laces, and when these laces became so tattered and worn that they could no longer be tied together, he often substituted heavy twine. In summer he wore soft and flexible Indian moccasins which he called "Bean shoes" because they came from the L. L. Bean company in Maine. Most of the time he wore coarse dark shirts and old denim trousers and a hunting coat and cap. When he tore the shirt or trousers on briars (which was often), he simply pinned the edges together with a small nail. His hunting coat, easily twenty-five years old, had never been washed or cleaned and was extremely stiff in texture.

He lived in the back country on a farm which had a dense woods with a creek running through it. It swarmed with small game, and this made it a paradise in his eyes, for he lived to hunt, and to study the creatures of the wilds. The farmhouse was a huge, old-fashioned structure with twelve or fourteen rooms, and its windows gleamed darkly with vacancy, for there was hardly any furniture in it, and no curtains or shades. It stood at the end of a long lane bordered by pines, about half a mile off a lonely country road, partly hidden by shrubs, vines, and shade trees. Empty, forlorn, aged and neglected in appearance, it had nevertheless been someone's pride and joy in the past, and still bore the marks of tasteful design and careful workmanship. The walls, strong and square, were of brick faded by years and weather. The long windows were set in pleasing frames that once had been white. The roof line was still sharp and true and it was easy to imagine supporting beams well seasoned, hand-hewn, unassailable and enduring.

At the back of the house was a flat-rock terrace shaded by grapevines, where stood a rusty pump. Beyond were other buildings, the hay barn, the sheep barn, the stables, a tool house, a carriage house, all empty and silent and deserted now except for the spiders that cast gossamer lines across the dusty panes, the wasps that built and daubed and sang, the bees that hummed their way in and out of small cracks where slivers of sunlight came through.

Behind these was a heavy farm gate, left open as though forgotten, leaning against a fence. Beyond it was a rutted farm lane scarred by wheels that had turned down its length in the spring thawing season, littered with remnants of dead herbage from the previous fall, overgrown with weeds that had sprung up that summer. The lane passed between fields empty and uncultivated, crossed a spring-fed creek, and ended in a woods deep and dense, full of dimness and coolness and wildlife.

Bill had lived at this farm for some time before anybody knew the place was occupied. Then some berry-picking lads reported that a man went in and out of the empty house, drank water from the rusty pump, worked in the silent garden. At the same time, the mail carrier stopped at the post-supported box with catalogues, newspapers, and magazines about wildlife or hunting. There were also infrequent letters which (he observed) seemed to come from banks or business firms and sometimes from historical societies.

Still, the neighbors asked, what sort of man would live in a house with no curtains at the windows and not even a collie dog to keep him company? The air of mystery about the whole situation gave rise to many curious speculations. Eventually, however, it was conceded that while Bill was a *character*; he was kindly and harmless and certainly had friends who were fine people, some even well known as naturalists or educators.

Among them was my great-uncle, who had attended school with Bill when they were boys. When I came to live in a Midwestern city some twenty miles from Bill's farm, this same uncle said to me, "Since you're so interested in natural history and the out-of-doors, you must meet him. He can teach you a lot."

Bill welcomed us hospitably to his empty house, where the boards in the floors creaked and echoed hollowly as you walked across them. Only two of the rooms were furnished in any manner whatsoever, and then so sparsely that you had to look twice to make sure they were not empty.

The kitchen was a small room which had a dusty window shaded by a gourd vine. Here stood a small, rusted cookstove with four holes in the top. In one corner stood *half* a chair . . . the lower half, of course. Against one windowpane was propped a large piece of a broken mirror. When his whiskers grew so long as to be uncomfortable, Bill went over to this piece of mirror and shaved, using a straight razor with terrifying abandon. Once, when an aching tooth had him half-frantic with pain, he went over to this piece of mirror and yanked the tooth out with his pliers.

The kitchen cupboard contained a few battered cooking utensils, ancient cutlery, some plates and cups. It also contained a whetstone, a pencil, a writing tablet, a pair of steel-rimmed spectacles, and several sharp skinning knives. A large medicinal calendar hung on the wall, and here Bill kept a sort of diary, writing the main event of each day with the stubby pencil. The diary might read:

MONDAY . . . The martins came back.
TUESDAY . . . Professer Boland was here.
WEDNESDAY . . . Had beans.

The living room served as Bill's bedroom. It had been a beautiful room once, but now it was dingy with age, and smelled of mice and dust. The paper hung in strips from cracked plaster. Over the fireplace later was a picture of me which he had ripped from a newspaper and nailed to the wall. Before the fireplace was a heap of old and dusty blankets. Bill spent all his winter evenings stretched out upon this repulsive bed, reading by the light of a kerosene lamp books of Indiana history, magazines dedicated to outdoor life, catalogues of hunting equipment. Probably no man in Indiana knew more about guns. His own collection, neatly racked at the far end of the room, was kept meticulously cleaned, oiled, polished, and inspected. He had other collections—birds' eggs neatly blown and catalogued, Indian relics, geological formations, moths.

Bill went hunting often and boasted that he had lived for years at a time without tasting store-bought meat. He shot rabbits and squirrels and ground hogs and quail and pheasant for food, caught fish and turtles. Every morning he was up at dawn. In winter he shoveled snow from the paths, cut wood, cooked his meals, and fed the birds. Then he made the rounds of feeding stations he had established to keep the woods creatures from starving during blizzards and ice storms. In summer he cut the grass, mended the fences, and tended his beautiful garden.

Bill loved all flowers, and planted, transplanted, and tended them with the greatest affection. When the weather was dry and the ground parched, he would spend a whole day carrying water to them. He had a collection of representative Indiana wild flowers and plants growing in shaded beds, some rare and hard to find, such as the cardinal flower, ginseng, the showy lady's-slipper. Along the garden fence he planted rows of sunflowers for the redbirds and corn for himself. When he gathered this corn, he parched it, Indian fashion, and ate it during the winter months. Sometimes he carried handfuls of it in his pockets when he went hunting. Fretfully, he deplored the passing of pemmican, until one day, tired of hearing about it, I said I would make some for him. And so I made small blocks of mincemeat which he gratefully accepted, and which he munched as he trudged.

About once a month he went into town to buy groceries, riding his bicycle the whole twenty miles. He needed no shopping list, for he had been buying the same items for so many years that he knew them by heart. Salt, sugar, pepper, coffee, canned milk, dried beans, crackers, and Fig Newtons. The Fig Newtons were his one luxury, his sole gastronomical indulgence.

Probably strangers who saw him at the market looked at him with pity, an old man ragged and unkempt who was carefully counting out change to pay for a few articles of food, but if they did their compassion was grossly misplaced, for Bill had a great deal of money. As the last member of his family, he had inherited large amounts of cash and property, also he owned some valuable guns, Indian relics, and natural-history collections. But he carried and spent almost nothing.

"The truth is," he often told me, "I jest don't never see anything I want to buy."

He had bought a new car back in 1912, but since he could not drive it across the woods or along the streams, he had scant use for it. Almost as good as new, it stood in the barn behind his house and was an object of great curiosity to most of the people who knew him. Now and then he drove it a few miles to see if it would still run, and years later he sold it to a collector for a sum that astonished him.

Though Bill spent most of his time alone, he was not lonely, for he found a consummate companionship in the out-of-doors. He was fiercely possessive toward his land and threatened to shoot on sight anyone who trespassed upon it, but his friends were welcomed affably. That summer, and others afterward, he suggested to my family that some of us, even my great-aunts, might escape the burning heat of town by spending some time at his farm. We had a brand-new tent which was as wonderful as any tent could be . . . with a floor, an awning, a screened door, two screened windows. It was bug-proof, mosquito-proof, rain-proof, snake-proof, everything but thunder-proof. And the farm was such a cool and pleasant place that we camped there not only that summer, but others.

"When the season opens, I'll take you hunting with me," Bill said, pleased to hear that I had a rifle of my own.

He went on, "You may *think* you've learned how to hunt and shoot, but you got to learn like an Indian to really *know!* You got to learn to walk like they did, and follow game like they did, and be really at home in the woods, not just a visitor. You wait! Before the season's over, I'll teach you to be an Indian!"

August came, bringing the squirrel season. Nights were clear and cool and full of stars. I slept deeply and peacefully while the soft wind carried the fragrance of Bill's garden across the fields, and stirred the leaves of the big elm overhead.

Some time before dawn I'd be awakened by the sound of his voice outside the door of the tent.

"Hey, Esther!" he'd whisper, in the way thunder whispers. "Come on! They'll be running in another half-hour!"

Nobody ever had to call me twice to go hunting. I would dress quickly, stuff my pockets with cartridges, a small mirror, comb, matches, handkerchief, a bottle of citronella. I have never owned any other clothes which I loved as much as my hunting clothes. I wore whipcord breeches, a thin shirt, a little denim hunting jacket, and (because the woods was usually so wet at dawn) knee-high boots of soft, flexible rubber.

In the darkness I would find my rifle and slip out of the tent without waking the others. Together Bill and I would start down the long farm lane to the woods, sometimes as early as three o'clock in the morning. Across our faces blew the cool, light wind that comes just before dawn, and the morning star burned white above us.

"Now, ain't that the purtiest sight in the world?" Bill would ask, in hushed wonder. "You know there never was a diamond, even in a king's crown, as purty as that. No, there ain't nothing that can beat the purtiness of nature." He would turn to me sternly then, and add, "Don't you ever go thinking store-jewelry is purtier than stars!"

As we walked along, I would tell him legends about the constellations. These he had never heard and they fascinated him, especially the story of Orion, the great hunter. He was always fascinated by legends and knew very unusual ones about pioneer Indiana and Wayne County. He told me about Lick Creek, in the hills to the south, where the deer came down to the salt lick in the early days. And how there was a ghost there that dropped down from the trees at night and settled on the shoulders of terrified travelers on the old Cincinnati-Centerville Highway, now thickets and briars. About Tecumseh and Johnny Appleseed and the Indians who lived and fought with Little Turtle. And he told me the story of the Great White Lizard, an animal the Indians had known and feared, but which had been almost extinct when the white man came to America. It was awful big, he said, and covered with a rough scaly hide, and it had short stout feet and a head like a horse. I heard the same story in Oklahoma, a legend of the Indians of the Southwest.

One of the strangest experiences I ever had was connected with a legend Bill told me.

It was during the summer and we were in the Lick Creek hills, looking for game and unusual plants, on a very hot day in August. In midafternoon, when I was tired and wanted to rest, Bill went on down the creek, leaving me at the bottom of a hill covered with trees. I stretched out in the shade and looked up at the leaves and drowsed for a while, then pulled a book from the pocket of my jacket and began to read.

Suddenly I had an eerie feeling that someone was watching me, and looked up quickly, just in time to see a man's face peering at me from around the trunk of a beech tree a little way up the hill. It vanished instantly, but not before I had seen that the face was very round and flushed and had a peculiar sleepy half-smiling expression. The incident startled me but I was not really frightened, supposing the man to be only a curious farmer.

I went back to my book, but the eerie feeling persisted. I looked up again, and again saw the face, this time peering around a different tree a little farther up the hill. Then suddenly it occurred to me that while I could see the man's features clearly, I could not see his shoulders at all! His face seemed to be in mid-air, unsupported, like a Halloween mask attached to a tree trunk.

A chill swept over me. I jumped to my feet, snatched my gun, and looked around for Bill. I could glimpse his bulky figure some distance away, moving soundlessly under the sycamores above the creek bed. I fled toward him, heedless of the noise I was making, crashing through the underbrush, recklessly trampling dry leaves and twigs.

He greeted me bitterly.

"What in tarnation do you think you're doing? You've scared all the game for miles!"

The sound of his familiar voice made everything seem normal again and I was instantly ashamed of my panic. Glancing over my shoulder, I saw that there was now no sign of the ruddy face, and began to think I had imagined the whole thing. The chills left me, the goose flesh vanished, and the day once more became hot and humid. I walked meekly at Bill's heels, and did not mention the experience.

Some weeks later, we were again hunting in Lick Creek. As we came to the tree-covered hill Bill said, "By the way, Esther, a settler had a cabin here once, one of the first settlers *in* here, I reckon. But the Indians got him . . . cut off his head. And for a long time afterward, folks claimed they seen him here, not *him* exactly, but jest his head—a-hanging in the air."

It was enough to make my teeth chatter. Perhaps it *was* a curious farmer peering at me that day, wearing a dark shirt which gave him protective coloring against the woods. But I certainly saw him clearly, and I did *not* see any shoulders.

Bill talked a lot about Indians. Nobody ever learned as much about the woods, he kept saying, and you had to be like them if you wanted to be a good hunter. You had to learn to sit absolutely positively *still,* to freeze suddenly in your own tracks, to keep your eyes open and know what was a-going on around you. That was the trouble with most folks. They thought that, out in the woods, there wasn't anything a-going on.

I learned to freeze against a tree so that my shadow became a part of it, to walk the woods in utter silence, slipping one foot ahead of the other, rolling my soles in order to avoid breaking twigs. To notice instantly the smallest movement . . . the fall of a leaf, the flutter of a bird's wing, the jump of a grasshopper. To quickly recognize a squirrel's summer nest (which Bill said many a hunter couldn't tell from a crow's nest), to know a den tree and a fox squirrel's bark.

Bill had spent years studying squirrels and taught me hunting tricks I had never heard from anyone else or seen in print. I learned how to make a fox squirrel look out of his den or nest, how to create a sound that would draw him near me, how to cause a moving squirrel to halt and lift his head.

"Then you can shoot him right through the eye," Bill told me. "And if you can't shoot a squirrel through the eye, you'd better go home."

But I shall reveal none of these things, for despite growing up with a gun in my hand, I deplore all unnecessary destruction of wildlife and despise the ways of most hunters. Bill taught me to have a very low opinion of the "average hunter" who sallies forth untrained and unskilled, endangering himself and all others with his blundering. Bill believed that hunting licenses, like driving licenses, should be issued only to qualified persons who had learned the basic rules and could pass a test.

The "average hunter" (he told me) seldom has had proper training and often does not even know how to aim a gun correctly. He is likely to carry it with the muzzle in his face, or in somebody else's face, and may even point it at another person as a huge joke. He loads it before leaving home, whereas a competent hunter loads a gun only in the field. He takes little notice of the number of shells he puts into a repeater, and does not make certain that all have been accounted for when the gun is unloaded.

He shoots uphill and downhill and across woodlands, though he cannot possibly know what may be above him, below him, or out of sight beyond some trees. (Many farm animals have been killed by such hunters.) He shoots at rocks and into streams, unaware that the bullet might ricochet and kill him or his companion. He shoots without seeing his target clearly, and this often leads to tragedy. ("I saw something in the bushes and fired. I never thought it was my buddy. . . .") He carries his gun cocked, or off safety, and playfully snaps the trigger when the magazine is empty. He climbs fences while carrying the gun, or perhaps tries to drag it through the wire. He neglects to clean and oil it after use, and allows it to become ruined by rust and dirt.

He hunts on other people's farms without permission and, even *with* permission, leaves gates open and lets livestock out, cuts costly fences to let hunting dogs through. In the woods he is equally unscrupulous, does not concern himself with making a "clean kill" but shoots game-animals in any way he can, often leaving them to drag themselves into the underbrush and bleed to death with legs broken, lungs torn by shot, eyes blinded by agony. Finding no squirrels (usually through his own ignorance of hunting techniques), he will unhesitatingly shoot through a nest, often killing or maiming a nursing mother whose young then starve, are destroyed by predators, or eaten alive by parasites. Such hunters may not even want the game they have managed to take, or know how to clean and use it. They can be counted, not among considerate and conscientious sportsmen, but among the human varmints who enjoy killing for its own sake, and derive a sense of personal accomplishment from seeing a terrified little creature ripped to death by vicious dogs.

Bill did not blame "average hunters" for their poor performance in the field as much as he blamed their mothers. He said he had observed that many mothers who quickly teach their sons to know and avoid the hazards of fire, traffic, poisons, and suspicious strangers will allow them to grow up regarding guns as toys or, just as bad, as grim weapons designed only for killing. Both attitudes, he said, were to be deplored. A child who finds a real gun is certain to pull the trigger if he has been taught to think of guns as playthings, and such tragedies happen again and again . . . have been happening for years. And a child who has not been taught to regard a gun properly when he is young, is most unlikely to handle it properly when he is older.

He was always baffled by mothers who answered a boy's very natural interest in marksmanship with, "That's too dangerous a hobby for you now. Wait till you're older," and then gave the boy a rifle on his sixteenth birthday with perfect confidence. Of course the boy knew no more about it than when he was ten, and was in quite as much danger, perhaps more, because he might take it out alone, was likely to resent or refuse supervision.

Shooting skills are valued and recognized as desirable by the majority of youth leaders, and may be developed at rifle ranges, skeet and trap shoots, gun clubs, youth competitions. Bill taught many boys to shoot, gave them lessons in the proper handling of guns, in gun safety and sportsmanship, laws and rules made to protect human life and manage game. His methods were much like those used by the Boy Scouts. His training was strict, however, and he did not permit the boys to hunt until they were qualified. Then he urged them never to kill harmless birds or animals, and to take no game except for the table.

There are many areas, of course, in which hunting is less a

sport than a necessity—for food, for the protection of crops, gardens, livestock, even human life. State conservation departments encourage hunting in order to maintain a "balance of nature," and there are times when the population of skunks, foxes, and other infected animals must be reduced in order to prevent the spread of rabies. But the wanton killing of wildlife is inexcusable, and though I had shot, skinned, cleaned, and cooked game many times, I came to avoid the killing of *any* wildlife except really vicious predators such as weasels, which slaughter and maim in bloodthirsty joy.

Now that he was older, Bill confined his hunting to the smaller types of game, such as quail, pheasant, rabbits, and squirrels. He had a special interest in squirrels and had spent something like sixty years watching them in the woods, studying their ways, their homes, their manner of foraging, mating, feeding, training their young, fighting, hiding, nesting, and moving.

Once, in a book about mammals, he showed me the picture of a tarsier.

"Says here," he told me, "that the t-a-r-s-i-e-r is a rare animal. But fellers spend all kinds of time studying it, finding out about it, even though it lives hunderds of miles away in a place nobody ever heard tell of . . . S-u-m-a-t-r-a. And I'll just bet American naturalists know more about *it* than they know about our common fox squirrel! You can talk to perfessers, and read books, and send for bulletins till you're blue in the face, and you won't find more'n a page about these animals that live right here in our own state!"

The fact that so many Indiana people were unaware of the wildlife and woodlore about them was a sad thing to Bill, and when a fourth-grade teacher of his acquaintance seemed surprised to hear that skunks eat hornets and bees, he was shocked.

"You'd think just *anybody* would know *that!*" he told me.

Among other things you'd think just *anybody* would know (according to Bill) were:

That baby bees have nurses.
That snakes "hear" with their tongues.
That newborn possums are no larger than lima beans.
That woodchucks manicure their nails.
That chipmunks cut off the rough edges of nuts before packing the nuts into their tender mouths.
That ants have funerals for their queens.
That a mink may float on a river curled up and sound asleep.

After years of studying the woods and its creatures and almost a lifetime of following game, Bill had come to the conclusion that the fox squirrel is one of the most interesting, intelligent, and appealing animals alive. And I doubt that anybody ever lived who knew more about them.

Fox squirrels, he said, were migratory creatures and didn't always stay in the same place all summer, but followed food and water supplies. When the weather was good and they had plenty to eat and drink, they'd stay within a mile or so of their dens. Squirrels liked to be in familiar territory where they could streak to their homes, or some other known hiding place, if they were hunted or pursued. However, when the green corn came on, or the nuts were ready, squirrels might range as far as eight or ten miles in their foraging, especially the males. Females were usually in the nest with young during late summer and early fall, unless they were young ones that had not yet mated.

During droughts, when the countryside was scorched and blistering hot, when their food lacked moisture and the berry or nut crop had failed, squirrels might move to foraging grounds a long distance away. Migrating squirrels could be identified by their scrawny bodies and scrubby tails worn thin by brambles, very different from the thick bushy tails of the natives. Hunters called them "travelers" and were disappointed when they shot one because it was too thin to make a good meal.

Some squirrels lived in tree-dens all the year round. Others built cool and pleasant leaf-nests in the treetops during summer, and returned to the warmer and more sheltered dens in winter. Their nesting places were often too high and too well concealed to be seen from the ground, but Bill insisted that you could locate them by smell.

"Primitive fellers smelled out game," he told me, "and we can too, if we try. We still got the same senses *they* had! We just don't use 'em."

To locate den trees and fresh squirrel tracks, you must first have their particular scent fixed in your memory forever, he explained, and persuaded me to inhale deeply the smell of fur and blood and warm flesh from an animal newly shot.

"You'll never forget it," he assured me, "and you'll always know it when you meet it in the woods."

Sometimes I thought I could detect the scent of a den tree on mornings when the woods were extremely wet, but the ability to "smell out game" claimed by many old hunters could never be claimed by me. The scents of a skunk and a fox were the only ones I could identify easily.

Fox squirrels, Bill told me, will start running the woods at dawn, partly to feed, partly to get warm. Even in hot August weather, the woods are extremely cold at dawn because the dew is so heavy. (And many a time, Bill and I were drenched from head to foot, shivering with chill, and looking as if we'd been washed up on a high tide.) Fox squirrels hate being wet, he said, and will often be seen lying on a branch in the benevolent morning sun, getting dry and comfortable. (We, too, were dry and comfortable after the sun rose, bringing the heat of the day.)

They dislike really hot sun, however, and stop feeding by nine or so, at least in our area, to retire to the coolness of their dens and nests. Since I seldom came upon a feeding squirrel after nine in the morning, I concluded that Bill was right, and they had their own means of telling time.

They'd run again about four in the afternoon, Bill said, and feed until dusk. He believed morning was the best time to hunt them, but other woodsmen equally skilled and experienced preferred late afternoon.

Any hunter with "young eyes" like mine ought to find it easy to hunt squirrels with a .22 rifle, he told me . . . and, if I had the right gun, to "bark" them. This method was used regularly by early hunters who carried muzzle-loaders. They shot, not the animal, but the "bark" (perhaps a branch) on which it lay, and the concussion brought it down.

Most men and boys who own guns have shot squirrels occasionally, but the true Squirrel Hunters in the hills of Indiana, Ohio, and Kentucky are a clan unto themselves, and as far removed from the casual hunter as Nimrod, Esau, and Hiawatha.

These men share an intense love and understanding of the hills and woodlands where many of them (but by no means all) were born. To them, hunting is as inseparable from the seasons of life and living as are snow, wild geese, spring rain, autumn leaves, youth, and old age.

They know the back country as it has been known before them only by the Indians and the first pioneers . . . or by the animals. For just as a wild animal knows his own territory intimately, so does the true squirrel hunter. These men are acquainted with every path, every tree, every waterfall within miles, with the runs of rabbits, the dens of foxes, the roosts of crows and vultures, the haunts of mink and pheasant, the beds of herbs and flowering plants, the sites of fruit- and nut-bearing trees.

They climb immense hills, explore caves and ledges and streams and ravines, crawl beneath coarse and tangled growth, pass through forests and thickets and swamps in a world singularly their own. It is a world remote and sometimes almost unknown to the town-and-city dwellers of their states who, beholding it from the ease of a superhighway, think of it only as "beautiful scenery."

The contributions of the squirrel hunters are not to be underestimated, for they have shared significant observations, experiences, and discoveries with professional people—naturalists, educators, writers, and others. And their knowledge of the wilds is valuable in other ways. Sometimes, for instance, a plane crashes in these hills and is hidden in a deep ravine or by heavy foliage. But even if a long and intense search on the part of the authorities has failed to locate it, they know that when the "season" opens, the squirrel hunters will find and report the wreckage, for there is no region however wild and remote through which they do not pass.

Yet their long and often rugged hunts are not for squirrel meat alone, or for the love of shooting, or even because bringing home game can fill them with a sense of superiority . . . for any real hunter brings home game. Instead, they are motivated by a love of wildlife and nature which, in their environment, can be consummated in no other way. It is a pattern men have followed for thousands of years: *I will lift mine eyes unto the hills. . . .*

Not even Bill could give articulate expression to this feeling, but it was a feeling he wanted me to share and he never ceased teaching me the ways and wonders of the woods. As we trudged down the lane he would keep reminding me, "Now, remember . . . to get a squirrel, you got to be smarter than *he* is! Don't laugh . . . it's the truth. You've just got no idea how smart a squirrel really *is!* If you expect to see one, you've got to sit quiet and wait till he thinks you've gone. Course, he may be watching you and if that's the case, you'll never see him a-tall, on account of he'll lay quiet till he *knows* you've gone. Any unusual sound you make will warn him about you. So don't crackle no twigs, nor strike no matches, nor slap no skeeters. Sit *still!* And if you reach for your gun, reach easy-like, don't grab and jerk. Squirrels can see sudden movements in the woods just like we can, only a lot better. We got awful poor eyes and ears and noses, Esther, compared to the wild things. Find out where a squirrel is feeding, and there he'll *be*, sometimes too busy and hungry to notice you, sometimes making so much noise of his own that it covers your tracks. This time of year, maybe it's walnuts they're cutting on, maybe it's corn."

As we entered the woods we would separate, Bill taking one side and I the other, and he would repeat the familiar warning, "*Be careful of your hands!*" For he frowned blackly upon my impulsive habit of reaching out, with bare hands, to seize or examine whatever I found interesting.

"Don't poke into no logs nor tree-holes nor ledges nor bunches of things!" he would scold.

A cluster of wild grapes might harbor a hornet or a wasp. Spiders often lurked in a clump of wild fern, bees in summer blossoms or in the cavities of trees, a rabid skunk in a log, a snapping turtle under a limestone ledge in the creek.

"And you never saw Turtle Ketchers that wasn't missing some of their fingers!" he would remind me.

But we didn't have to worry about poisonous snakes, at least not in our particular locality.

One morning he shot an enormous fox squirrel and showed me that it had unusually glossy and beautiful fur. On Christmas, he gave me the pelt as a gift, nicely cured and wadded into a piece of faded Christmas paper with a frayed red ribbon tied around it.

"I thought this would give you a start," he explained, beaming proudly. "You know, if you keep right on saving them, you can have a nice coat."

"Well, I've got one cuff," I thought, with a dubious look at the squirrel skin.

Bill's gifts to his friends were wholly unpredictable, to say the least. Now and then, during the winter months, the postman would bring me a postcard yellow with age and adorned with a view of something like *Main Street, 1902,* probably from Bill's attic. On the back would be written such a message as: *Coming to town Tuesday. Will stop around 4* P.M. *with a PRESENT!*

Usually, I was filled with apprehension, not knowing what to expect. It might be some freshly parched corn for me to munch, while thinking nervously of dental bills. Once it was a bag of rancid pork cracklings, which I had to eat at once lest his feelings be hurt. But in autumn it was a charming gift from the woods—freshly gathered bittersweet or hickory nuts, perhaps a swallowtail butterfly or a beautiful luna moth.

Then, one frosty morning, he brought me a white-faced hornet's nest, a great oval of tough light-gray paper. He had shot it down for me the day before, sending a bullet through the branch on which it was built and from which it hung.

"You don't often see anything more interesting," he told me.

Assuring me that the hornets had left it and there was nothing to fear, he hung it near my desk, where it remained for a long time, drawing comments both curious and caustic from my friends. But even the caustic ones lingered on, fascinated when they examined it, and in the end they agreed that they didn't often see anything more interesting.

II Bill and I hunted together for several years, tramping over frozen fields when the snow had stopped and the sun had come out, slipping through midsummer woodlands damp and sweet and cool. Bill was very strict about my guns, made sure that I kept them oiled and immaculately clean. He didn't want me to become dependent upon telescope sights, which he said were for "big-game hunters, poor shots, and old fellers," and insisted that I learn to hold my rifle on a target, steady and still, without using a strap. He put full buckhorn sights on my Winchester and made me practice until I could split the *edge* of a piece of cardboard at thirty-six feet. With something like an evil chuckle, he taught me such tricks as "how to shoot with your sights covered" . . . a gross deception that was awe-inspiring to uninitiated bystanders, as it appeared to be a feat of incredible skill. (Actually, it was pure trickery, accomplished by shooting with both eyes open.)

Sometimes, as we walked along in summer, Bill would stoop and pick a blossom so tiny that I would never have seen it at all. He would find diminutive flowers no larger than the head of a pin and show them to me.

"Just look!" he'd say. "So purty and delicate-like! Nope, there ain't nothing can beat the purtiness of nature."

He would make small colorful bouquets and fasten them

in the buttonhole of his denim shirt pocket, perhaps blue St. Mary asters and pink knotweed. (Bill often said that if knotweed was sold in flower shops, folks would be willing to pay a mighty purty penny for it.) Once he brought in a cluster of blossoms so small that he put it in a rusty thimble full of water.

Often he would pick up arrowheads and show me which were for hunting and which for war.

"Just think," he'd say, awed, "some Indian's hands shaped this arrowhead. Wonder what he looked like, don't you? Wonder what he thought about when he done it. Maybe he stood right here under these same oaks. . . ."

He showed me a hummingbird's nest, with eggs smaller than peas.

"I tell you," he would say regretfully, "people live and die and never learn to see the Little Things."

Because he taught me to look for them, I have seen unforgettable bits of beauty and wonder. Once I watched a shiny black cricket sing gloriously as he sat upon a bright-red toadstool lined with fluted chartreuse green. Once I saw an enormous green toad with bright red eyes, like an evil creature out of a fairy tale. I have watched a mother squirrel moving her babies, carrying them by the skin of their small soft stomachs. I have seen a mother possum with her little ones riding on her back, clinging to her tail for support as she held it bent rigidly above them. Many times, on tawny fall days, I have looked up into the peeled white branches of giant sycamores and seen garlands of bittersweet swaying in the wind against a bright blue sky. I have seen a Painted Lady butterfly on a pink star-thistle, a yellow finch singing in a clump of bright blue chicory, wild geese flying into a red dawn, the courting dance of the golden flicker.

One day I came upon a large black evil-looking spider in a huge web. As I watched, a young katydid crashed into the web and in a flash, the spider was upon it, had wrapped it tightly in strands of webbing. I was sorry for the little katydid, bound and helpless, and knew the spider was now ready to end its life with a vicious bite, and so leaned forward and freed it with my rifle barrel. It seemed stunned, and some time passed before it was able to leap away. I felt that the spider was glaring at me, hating me, and so I made a face at it and went my way.

No doubt I had absorbed Bill's habit of seeing in all woods creatures individual characteristics and personalities. He would say to me, "Don't go too close to them hornets, Esther. They've got meaner faces than most." He would say, "Tiptoe away from that toad, please. Can't you see he's looking anxious? They're no worse feeling than to be anxious!"

Or he would tell me, "No, *this* is the tree for sassafras! I've come to it every year, and it knows me. I reckon it'd feel real bad if I went to a different one." And sometimes, after carefully arranging wild flowers in an old cracked cup, "Now, don't move any of 'em . . . you hear? I've got them fixed just the way they *want* to be!"

Bill was interested in every living thing. When he hunted beyond his own lands, often on the farms of his cronies, and crossed meadows where animals were grazing or barnyard flocks feeding, he would stop to give them little treats and make friends with them. It was not unusual to see him ambling along, his gun on his arm, a friendly gander honking at his heels, a contented lamb trotting on one side of him, and a shy little white-faced calf on the other.

He was utterly enchanted by a beautiful colt in one of the pastures, carried apples and sugar to it, talked to it solemnly as they walked on together. And it was indeed fascinating to see this old hunter trudging across the meadow accompanied by a colt with its head hanging over his shoulder.

One beautiful summer day the colt felt so merry that it galloped, spun, romped, leaped, and kicked up its heels. But these joyful antics were carried on too close to Bill, and the colt accidently kicked his leg. It was a terrific blow, and Bill collapsed in pain, believing his leg broken, while the colt came to an abrupt halt beside him.

"Poor feller," Bill told me afterward. "He didn't aim to hurt me, but he knowed he had, and he nuzzled me and nickered and whinnied, just carried on. I felt awful sorry for him. I could see he was all broke up. . . ."

Bill at last managed to stagger within hailing distance of the farmhouse, but his leg was badly bruised, and it was some time before he could hunt again.

Among other things, Bill taught me a lot about the wild flowers that grow in Indiana. Most people don't know, he said, that few of them are native flowers. Pioneer Indiana was a dense wilderness, dark and damp and full of swamplands. The flowers that grew in the dimness and dampness could not live in the sun, and so vanished with the trees. Settlers brought new ones, sometimes on purpose, sometimes by accident. They packed their belongings in hay and straw from European fields, and the seeds of European plants became immigrants too, and flourished here with the families that fetched them in.

Among the so-called "Indiana wild flowers" which belong to the immigrant group are: dandelions, bouncing Bet, Queen Anne's lace, the common field daisy, the tawny lily that grows along the country roadsides and blooms in June. Among the native blossoms still to be found are ironweed, pokeberry, the wild rose, and the rare cardinal flower.

Bill knew where every wild flower grew, and we would come home in spring with armloads of wake-robins (white trilliums), bunches of white, yellow, blue, and purple violets. We gathered Dutchman's breeches, squirrel corn, columbines, cowslips, and the blossoms of dogwood, locust, hawthorne, and redbud trees.

In summer and early fall, meeting the familiar flowers again was pert-near as good as a family reunion, Bill said. We came upon the bloom of the wild bergamot, pink or red or purple, trumpet vine, New England asters, dayflowers, chicory, yarrow, Turk's-cap lilies, meadowsweet, butterfly weed, and countless others.

Bill would point out the plants that were poisonous and dangerous, and those used by settlers and Indians for healing, such as mullein, camomile, plantain, and the beautiful Joe-Pye weed, named for a famous Indian medicine man. He taught me to treat stings and bites with juice from the crushed leaves of the jewel weed (wild touch-me-not) which grew in moist woodlands. Its fragile blossoms looked like orange or yellow trumpets from fairyland.

In fall he was eager to know whether woodland fruits were plentiful—bunchberries, partridgeberries, haw apples, dogwood fruit, rose berries, staghorn sumac, ground cherries, and others. For in winter, the birds depended upon them for food. We gathered hickory nuts, walnuts, persimmons, and rich meaty pawpaws. Wild grapes hung in thick blue clusters along rail fences, and from trees where vines had climbed. I took them home and made them into a tart and delicious jelly.

Bill said the gray haze which hung upon the horizon in Indian summer was smoke from the council fires of Indian ghosts.

"Then the spirits of the old chiefs come back," he said, almost believing it, "and look in sadness at the lands we stole away from them, and in shame at what we done, cutting away the forests and turning the good rich earth to dust."

One tawny October day, as we stood upon a hilltop, he pointed across the valley where frost had turned the leaves to gold and scarlet against a bright blue sky.

"Folks say I'm stingy," he told me. "They can't understand why I don't fix my house up fancy, with purty pictures on the walls. Over there is my pictures, and money can't buy none like 'em."

Now and then he would tell me about his boyhood, when he had gone to school with a shy little lad called Willie. Willie was so susceptible to colds that his mother sent him to school with his head swathed in a shawl, a matter of great amusement to Bill and other hatless boys having snowfights in the drifts.

"You mustn't laugh at Willie!" Bill's mother scolded. "He might grow up to be smarter than you!"

"And today," Bill told me, with awed respect, "he's President-Amertus of the college."

Often, very often, he talked about his wife. He had been married when he was very young, but the marriage had not lasted. His wife had brown hair like mine, he said, and was little like me. I had heard that she was a delicate girl who could not get used to parched corn and wild game and no comforts (there wasn't even an inside pump). But that was something Bill never understood.

"I don't know why she left me," he would say sadly. "I just don't know. Why I got her the finest rifle money could buy, and a little pair of hunting boots, special made. . . ."

It never ceased to bewilder him.

When we came back to the farmhouse after a morning of hunting, I was usually very hungry, but I did not mention this right away. If I had, Bill would have insisted that I eat some of the awful brews he cooked in his wretched little kitchen, things like rabbit stew mixed with corn. I would not have touched anything he cooked, for too often I had seen him dispose of fallen ashes or soot by hastily stirring them into the beans. So when my family and I were spending the day with him, we would bring our own food, dishes, and utensils, inviting Bill to join us. Our meals would be picnics under the trees in summer, campfire cookouts at the edge of the woods in fall. Bill just took it for granted (and with a great deal of satisfaction) that I preferred to eat out-of-doors like an Indian.

One summer morning he said to me, "Esther, do you reckon you could cook me some old-fashioned saloon turtle soup?"

Saloon times, he added, were the good old days, and he gave me a lengthy, nostalgic description of the free lunch. There used to be an old German saloonkeeper in the south end of town (my town) who made the best turtle soup in the world, and Bill had his recipe. If he got a turtle, could I make the soup?

I said I would try, so he gave me the sacred formula. It was written on an aged scrap of paper and long preserved in a mildewed wallet concealed in a pitcher. It said:

Lew's Turtle Soup

Clean and cut up a good-size turtle. Put in a good-size kettle with two or three pieces of the shell, washed and cleaned good. Cover over with water and boil slow till the meat come off of the bones. Then take out the meat, bones, and shell.

Into the turtle broth put:

2 pounds of potatoes (chopped up small)
1 onion, good size (chopped up small)
1 teaspoon whole cloves
½ teaspoon red pepper
1 whole lemon (sliced, seeds took out)
½ pound cabbage (cut up some)
#2 can tomatoes
#2 can peas
#2 can corn
enough salt to taste right

While these cook in the broth, put 2 heaped-up Tablespoons flour in a small-size iron skillet. Cook over low fire until flour turns good and brown. *Stir all the time.* Take off and add a little broth, enough to make a smooth gravy. Then pour this in soup.

Cook till vegetables are done. To eat: Put some turtle meat in the bottom of a big bowl and cover with hot soup. Yum, yum!

We spent the next two or three days looking for a turtle but did not find one. As we walked up and down, Bill became thirsty and drank from the creek, a sight which horrified me.

"Done it all my life!" he said calmly, when I protested. Then he added, "You keep on listening to them doctors, and you'll never see twenty-five!"

One fruitless morning he decided the weather wasn't right for turtles and we'd have to get one in town, from some folks he knew who were "perfessional turtle ketchers" and brought them up from the southern part of the state. I was just learning to drive, but he seemed to have no apprehensions about my dubious skill, so I drove him into town, pathetically grateful for his silence when I twice killed the motor and once grazed a "Danger" sign on a curve. He directed me to a tumble-down house swarming with hound-dogs and children, the hound-dogs looking much brighter than the children. A slatternly woman said yes, they had nice fresh turtles, and took us to the cellar to see them. A stream of water had been turned into this dark and dank place, and here were the turtles, great snapping brutes covered with mud and slime, crawling on the edge of a wet coal pile.

Bill carefully selected the largest one and held him up snapping, struggling, and dripping dirty water and coal dust.

"Yum, yum!" he said appreciatively. "Won't he taste good?"

I swallowed convulsively and couldn't bear to look. Bill paid the woman happily, and I asked her for something in which to carry the turtle. She said haughtily that if folks wanted tow-sacks they'd have to fetch 'em theirselves!

All the way back to the farm Bill sat beside me holding and gloating over the struggling turtle, which so unnerved me by snapping at my knees that I narrowly missed a head-on crash with the U.S. mail. As soon as we arrived, he killed and cleaned it and I washed it about a hundred times at the pump. To my surprise the meat looked white and firm and tender, even appetizing. When I finished cooking it, even my family liked this alien brew and Bill ate at least a gallon of it.

"You ought to be awful proud," he told me solemnly. "I

bet there's not many girls in this county can make real saloon turtle soup!"

He was so grateful that he planned a surprise for me, a ride in the 1912 automobile. Being seated on the front seat of this invention was about as enviable an experience as being seated on a ducking stool, for at that time old cars were still *old cars* and had not yet attained the status of treasured antiques. As we passed, people stared, pointed, screamed, called to each other, and rocked with ribald laughter, but Bill noticed none of this.

"Runs right good," he kept saying. "I never drive it more'n once a year, though. Too much bother."

Here was a car that the owner didn't even drive to church, because the owner didn't *go* to church! It looked as good as new, its only blemish being a back window from which the isinglass was missing. Bill laid his shotgun on the floor and we chugged to the country store two miles up the road, and then to the Far Woods where he intended to hunt. He bought three boxes of Fig Newtons and offered me one, but I would as soon have eaten grit wrapped in cardboard, so he ate them all himself.

"Ain't likely I'll ever take this auto out again," he said, as we went along. "I . . . I just don't trust myself to drive no more. . . ."

His voice broke and I knew he was thinking about his eyes. Lately he had talked a lot about them. He knew they were failing, he said, and his sight was going. He had bought new glasses and gone twice to see an oculist, but nothing seemed to help.

"If . . . if I have to be blind, then I don't see no reason to go on living," he told me. "Life to me is the woods and the wild things and the purtiness of nature. I ain't said much, but I know . . . I know. My gun sights don't look right to me, and when I try to shoot, everything's a blur. . . ."

My heart ached with pity, but before I could say as much

as a hopeful word, a squirrel leaped upon a stump in a field we were passing. It was yards away and I did not dream he could see it, but in a flash he slammed on his brakes, snatched his gun, and aimed through the back window. *Wham!* The squirrel fell dead. I dashed the tears from my eyes and glared at Bill and never worried about his eyes again.

I, too, loved to shoot, but I didn't want to shoot living things. My love of "hunting" was really a love of the woods, the wildlife I watched there, the out-of-doors. Many times I sat under a tree with my rifle across my knees and watched baby squirrels playing hide-and-seek, chasing each other around a tree trunk. It was a sort of instinct they had, Bill said, something they all did.

One would hide at one side of the tree until another slyly came hunting and found him. Then they would be off together, streaking joyously up and down and around and around, as though laughing with glee.

I would watch an older squirrel lying on a branch, seeking the warmth of the morning sun, ever tensed and fearful, ever in danger, never knowing peace or safety. I would lie in a deep bed of leaves in the autumn woods and see baby rabbits hopping and playing around me. Once a small cottontail, fleeing from a hunter, ran right across me. A little ground hog (one of the cutest woods creatures) came crashing through the underbrush and took refuge in the hollow log on which I was sitting, running from a hunter with a shotgun. In the stillness that followed, I could hear the frightened little animal panting for breath, and could imagine the wild beating of his little heart.

Birds, being less hunted, were less fearful and easier to observe. There were mourning doves, so beautiful and so stupid, their nests so ridiculous that the eggs often fell out. (In back-country Indiana an inept woman is sometimes said to be "dumb as a dove.") There were cardinals and bluebirds and cedar waxwings, the mellow-throated meadow lark, the arrogant jay, the cute tufted titmouse, the chickadee. All day I heard song sparrows and indigo buntings and wild finches, saw the red-headed woodpecker attacking a tree trunk, watched the funny disheveled kingfisher along the creek. In early evening the incredibly lovely song of the wood thrush echoed through the first hush. As the sun went down I would hear the "bobwhite" call of the quail, the plaintive cry of a distant killdeer, the voices of mockingbirds and red-wing blackbirds, the liquid notes of a robin. When dusk came on, the woods grew dark and still and there would linger only the sad call of the little peewee, surely one of the loneliest sounds in the world.

One evening, when I was in the woods alone, I heard the raucous voice of a flicker nearby. The flicker is one of Indiana's most interesting birds, so I dropped between some bushes and lay flat upon the ground, watching for it. It was trying to go home but like all wild creatures, was cautious and afraid. It would call a long time and then move a little nearer an old dead beech.

I saw that the beech was a sort of flicker apartment house, drilled to the very top with neat round holes. After a long time, during which the sun went down, the bird drew closer and at last dared to fly into a hole halfway up the trunk. As twilight came on, it grew bolder and sat squarely in front of the hole, looking out. Presently it nodded like a drowsy old lady and went to sleep, its head hanging over the rim. Other flickers came home and went to roost in the beech tree, but this one did not awaken. The twilight deepened, Arcturus came out, and frogs began to call from a nearby swamp. I rose carefully, without any noise, picked up my rifle, and started up the path. As I looked back, I saw that the tired little flicker was still there, sound asleep, with its little red-spotted head hanging out of the hole.

I was fascinated by crows, admired their intelligence and cunning, and, from Bill, learned the meaning of their calls.

Crows are the town criers of the woods, and have their own scouts and sentinels that are ever alert to danger, ever on guard against intruders. Many a time, though I froze against a tree trunk in utter silence and shadow, a sentinel crow found me and his raucous voice spread the alarm throughout the woods. "*Caw! Caw! Caw! Caw!*" four short, loud, and warning syllables. Crows have calls of greeting, calls of command, danger, love, sorrow, and others.

Sometimes when I hunted alone I would stay in the woods until long after sunset and come home at moonrise, hearing the voices of the funny little "eight owls" whose calls hold eight notes, never more. And rarely (though often enough for me) I would hear the ominous voice of the great horned owl deep in the darkening thicket, fierce and menacing. "Hoo! Hoo! Hoo-hooooooo!" I pictured it hunched upon a dead limb, thought of its huge steel-like claws, its gleaming yellow eyes, its swift and silent strike—and for an instant, knew something of the terror that little woods creatures must feel at the sound of its voice.

When I wanted to shoot (an urge that is almost a compulsion to gun-lovers), I would pick a safe and sheltered spot for target practice. Cardboard targets bored me, however, so I used another kind. In a valley down in the Lick Creek hills there was a gravel pit with a number of thorn trees growing in front of it. I would push the thorns through the holes in soda crackers and when the trees were abloom with these nice white targets, step back fifty feet and shoot them off.

But killing was another thing . . . and many a terrified little animal have I saved by begging Bill to let *me* shoot at it. Afterward, he would say in disgust, "I just don't understand how you can shoot an apple off a tree, and then go and miss a squirrel the size of a cow!"

I never told him how I felt about shooting things, for he would not have understood. To Bill, all game was fair game, put here for man to kill and eat, and nothing to be sentimental about. (Though when a passing hunter shot Skipper, his pet squirrel, Bill spent weeks in violent, incoherent, and profane outbursts of rage against the kind of lowdown trash who would kill a helpless fox squirrel.)

One day he said heavily, "I dunno, Esther. Seems to me you've lost heart some way." He shook his shaggy white head and answered sadly, "It's a sorry thing to lose a hunter's heart."

Sometimes, coming home at sunset, we would stop to rest from a long climb, sitting in the grass on a quiet hilltop, our rifles across our knees. We would look in silence across a valley, see clouds edged with glory, woodlands bright with fall, hear the distant calling of a dove or the sleepy song of a cardinal nesting in a wild grapevine. Bill professed no religion and probably never heard of William Cullen Bryant, yet in his lined and weathered face I saw reflected:

My heart is awed within me when I think
Of the great miracle that still goes on
In silence round me . . . the perpetual work
Of Thy creation finished, yet renewed
Forever. Written on Thy works I read
The lesson of Thine own eternity.

Bill would say, "When I'm too old and feeble to go to the woods and hills, my life is over." And when the time came, that was how it happened. Confined to a hospital room because of a heart ailment, he lay with his face to the open window, gazing out at the sky.

"I been thinking about my life," he told me, "and I guess that in all of it, there's only one thing I'm sorry for."

I moved uncomfortably, embarrassed and alarmed by his tone of utter contrition.

"Yes," he went on sadly, "there's one thing I done that I wish I hadn't done. *I worked two months once.* Inside, in a shop." He paused and added in accents of bitter regret, "Two months away from the woods!"

Later he said to me, "When I die, I don't want no sermon. I just want you to write me a poem, a nature-poem, and I want it buried with me. Promise."

I promised, not letting him see my tears, and when he was gone, I wrote:

Now let the earth, the gentle earth,
Of life so dear a part,
Into its sheltered rains and dawns
Receive a hunter's heart.

Now let the sky, where feathered clouds
Are written, scroll on scroll,
Into its miracle of stars
Receive a hunter's soul.

The holiness of dawn,
The benediction of a tree,
The requiem of cardinal songs
Be his eternity.

After that, whenever I thought of him, I could return for a little time to a part of my life that was forever ended. I could remember the sweet darkness of the early summer mornings, and the soft light wind that blew across the woods just before dawn. I could feel the rutted lane beneath my hunting boots, see the morning star burning white in the east, and hear his voice saying, "Don't you ever go thinking store-jewelry is purtier than stars!" I could feel the touch of my Winchester on my arm, like the touch of an old and beloved friend, and see again the gentle affection in the face of this colorful old man who was so proud of teaching me to be an Indian.

III From Bill I had learned a great deal about "woods talk" and could readily identify such sounds as the "go-away" protests of a catbird (uttered when an intruder came near her nest), the raspy help-call of a crow, the love-singing of a toad, the mating coquetry of a female squirrel, the alarm signal of a mother robin, and others. The language of wild things is clear and explicit to those who understand it, Bill said, though we hear very little of it at best because so many of the sounds are too high or too low for human ears.

He had told me more than once about the distress call of a squirrel, one of the most penetrating sounds in all nature, a shrill and despairing wail you never forgot, though like many animal sounds, it *could* be mistaken for the call of a bird. But in all the time I spent with him we never encountered it, and so I never really learned to identify it.

Years went by before I heard it at all. I was married to Lee, whom I had known since my girlhood, had a grown daughter, Jamie, and lived in a small Midwestern city on the National Road, where Lee was in business. Traffic roared past us all day, but there were lovely shade trees on our street, also shade trees and shrubs and bushes around the house, and so we managed to achieve an illusion of the country, even to lure wild birds and wild animals to our feeding shelf.

The years I spent at my desk writing and studying were not

unrewarding, but sometimes I felt like a lonely exile from a world loved and remembered, the familiar back country where clouds and rain and woods were an integral part of daily existence, lost to me now except through a glass literally. For the room in which I worked had a window so high and wide that to look out of it at all was to see a lovely expanse of sky fringed by leaves and vines.

I saw and heard the seasons go past this window in a parade of years. Spring came with a burst of redbud bloom, the leafing of the mulberry tree, the flash of a cardinal's wing. Summer meant warm and fragrant nights when crickets chirped in the grass, when the smell of honeysuckle came in on the wind, fireflies drifted past, and beyond them lightning flashed, far away. Fall brought a frosty wind rising, rising, a flurry of dead leaves against the pane, and the tawny light of a harvest moon. In winter, snow fell against this window, sometimes in gentle blanketing flakes, sometimes like mist whirled before a gale.

We had a small and very black puppy named Cricket, and she too loved this window. She would stand on the studio couch beneath it, her paws on the sill, her head turning rapidly from side to side as she looked upon such sights as are fascinating and wonderful to little cockers—the passing of a butterfly, the flutter of a bird's wing, the tumbling fall of a great yellow leaf in autumn.

We put a feeding shelf near this window and a birdbath nearby. Wild birds began to come from the trees along the streets, from the trees in the park not far away. After a while we came to know them as individuals with characteristic habits and personalities. There was a fat, solemn robin who never ran or hopped or sang. He was silent, morbid, solitary. In the birdbath he never fluttered his wings or tossed sprays of water into the air, but sat immersed up to his neck, soaking, not moving. Later he would fly to the fence and sit in the sun, dripping dry. He never shook himself even once, he just dripped. And so, for reasons completely obvious, we named him Drippy.

There was a funny, adolescent little cardinal who, instead of being sleek and graceful and trim like the others, was ragged and clumsy and unkempt. His voice held none of the liquid melody characteristic of cardinals, but had a funny rusty sound. But his heart was joyous, and on beautiful mornings he sometimes sang with such abandon that he completely lost his balance and fell over on his beak.

A pair of beautiful and devoted cardinals came to the feeding shelf every day, morning and evening. Mrs. Cardinal was a shy and timid little soul, nervous about leaving the shelter of the rosebushes. Her mate always preceded her with encouraging and reassuring little chirps. As they dined, he would turn the sunflower seeds over and over, until he found a particularly plump and appetizing one. Then he would crack it, extract the kernel, hop over, and place it in his wife's beak. Quite often they would "kiss" each other by touching beaks affectionately, and sometimes in spring they would sit side by side on a branch and sing to each other. Cardinals are usually devoted to their mates, the males tender and protective toward the females. Many times I have watched them feeding at sunset, in bushes or hedgerows; I never saw them feeding alone, but always in pairs. *Once*, however, I did encounter a male cardinal who was greedy and abusive, who wanted all the food for himself and beat his frightened little wife with his wings when she took as much as a seed for herself. But that is only further evidence, I suppose, that there is an unfeeling lout in every community.

The cardinal is the state bird of Indiana, and may be seen and heard everywhere. It is the male who is spectacularly red, brilliantly crested, and socially poised. The female is brownish-gray, with orange-red crest and beak, usually timid and retiring. Since many of these birds do not migrate, they came to our feeding shelf all winter, and once I saw a cardinal sitting and singing among the pink blossoms of a plum tree that was blooming in the snow. (In Japan the plum tree is known as a symbol of courage "because it puts forth flowers while snow is still on the ground.")

Other birds which came to our feeding shelf in the middle of town were the cute tufted titmouse (especially if we served nut meats), the bluejay, robin, mourning dove, chickadee, nuthatch, downy woodpecker, starling, and of course the ubiquitous pigeon. One spring Jamie hung out a small house with a sign on it that said *For Wrent*, and it was soon occupied by a pair of chattery fuss-budgets.

We found that a narrow, collapsible window screen (the kind set in a wooden frame) made an excellent feeding shelf because the rain passed through it and the food stayed fairly dry. Lee, my husband, fastened it to the sill so that we could raise the window and fill it, or clear it of snow, without having to go outside in severe weather.

There was a nest of starlings in the redbud tree, and they used our feeding shelf and birdbath extravagantly. Though they did not appear especially arrogant, the other birds quickly departed when they came and appeared to fear and shun them, probably because the starling is often guilty of purloining other birds' nesting places.

Most people abhor starlings, but we found them very interesting for their mimicry of native residents. Sometimes on an icy winter morning, Lee would waken me at dawn and motion toward the redbud tree outside the window and say, "Listen!" We would hear a titmouse, bluejay, crow, dove, mockingbird, meadow lark, indigo bunting, all imitated with amazing accuracy by a certain male starling.

I discovered his talents one cold December morning when I awoke to hear a cardinal's mating song. This was absurd, impossible! What cardinal would sing its mating song between Thanksgiving and Christmas instead of waiting until the last of February? Puzzled and curious, I sought out the source of this rippling melody and found our talented starling!

Once we thought we heard visitors talking just outside our window and got up and looked out only to see him busy with a new form of mimicry. He had learned to imitate people passing up and down the street, and his version sounded exactly like human voices mingled in indistinct conversation.

Starlings, considered valuable for their destruction of harmful insects, were brought here from Europe in 1890 and, like all pioneers, moved ever westward. The first to appear in Indiana were sighted in 1927. Their descendants, numbering thousands upon thousands, have come to be looked upon as pests because they gather on buildings and along city streets in winter, befoul trees and walls and sidewalks, and keep citizens awake with their constant twittering.

Our starlings, however, kept to themselves, caused us no trouble, and never took part in the raucous riots of their kind. Perhaps it was because they were warm, well fed, and therefore content with their lot. They had a cosy hole in the redbud tree, a birdbath full of fresh water, plenty of insects in summer supplemented by meat scraps and bits of suet in winter.

The starling is really a short-tailed blackbird whose commonest call is a wolf-whistle. In spring his beak turns yellow and his sleek black feathers, seen in the sun, reflect green and purple lights. In winter, protective coloring dims his glory. He appears duller, browner, and is speckled with white. Even his yellow beak becomes drab (he is the *only* blackbird with a yellow beak), but his spirit remains blithe and his musings articulate. On dark and dreary winter days, Lee and I felt immensely privileged to be awakened by the spring song of a meadow lark even though both the spring and the lark were still far away.

The boldest of our visitors was a male bluejay, large, beautiful, and arrogant. He would flash to the feeding shelf, chase the other birds away, and stuff himself until he could scarcely fly, especially if he found nut meats. Bluejays are notoriously ill-tempered, and if he came too early and found the feeder empty, he would fly into an absolute rage, scream wildly, and beat the windowpane with his wings.

Bill had always disliked bluejays because of their insolence and because they constantly molested the nests of other birds in summer, destroyed eggs and young.

"I caught one of them danged things after a robin's nest this morning," he told me once. "Picked up my gun and shot out his tail feathers."

"What did he do?" I asked.

"He flew off through the orchard yelling, '*Jesus! Jesus!*' Served him right."

Bluejays are all noisy, but sometimes their noise is mere exuberance. On beautiful spring mornings, when the air was so fresh and the sun so warm that every living thing felt happy, I have seen our bluejay fly back and forth over the house, back and forth, back and forth, screaming for pure joy.

Bluejays destroy many harmful insects, but they are vicious predators and may be seen in the wilds carrying and eating small snakes, frogs, mice, and baby birds. They took bits of raw meat from our feeder, as well as suet and nut meats, and were very fond of sunflower seeds. However, they lacked the cardinals' ability to crack and strip these seeds with their beaks. Like the tufted titmouse, the bluejay would seize one of these seeds in his beak and beat it against a hard surface until it cracked open and released the tender kernel. Sometimes in late summer, he would bring his youngsters, all beautiful and noisy, to share these kernels.

Bluejays are as alert as crows in detecting a stranger in the woods, and will warn all other creatures of his presence. Sometimes they will set upon him and torment him or drive him out, especially if the intruder is a squirrel or an owl, two creatures who seem to have incurred their undying hatred.

Whenever we heard the raucous and persistent screaming of

several bluejays, Bill would say, "Let's go and find out what they've treed!" Very often it was an owl roused from his sleep and forced to seek asylum elsewhere, but I always thought he seemed more bored than afraid.

Inexperienced hunters who hear a bluejay shrieking in the woods attach little significance to the sound, do not know that he has sent the game scurrying for cover, and wonder why they come home without a shot fired. (As a matter of fact, when you consider the many bird and animal sentinels that keep watch and give alarms, it is surprising that inexperienced hunters ever see any game at all. Rabbits thump the ground to signal danger, beavers slap the water with their tails, woodchucks whistle, chipmunks chirp, red squirrels chatter, robins scold, and so on.)

Though the bluejay possesses a raucous voice, he is also capable of a song of such lyrical beauty that those who hear it for the first time stare in amazement, unable to believe that it came from this callous, arrogant, and profane creature of the woods.

If Shakespeare had been born in Indiana, he would not have written, "*It was the lark, the herald of the morn . . . ,*" for in Indiana, the herald of the morn is the robin. While the sky is still dark, long before the colors of the sunrise are seen, while the first pale light glimmers in the east, a single beautiful liquid note is heard, whether in city, village, or woodland, the matin of the robin. It is followed, usually, by the voice of a cardinal; then a whole chorus of bird songs rises to salute the new day.

Every year, in late summer, the parent birds that lived around us brought their young to our fence or bushes or trees in an attempt to lure them to the feeding shelf and teach them to eat. I marveled at their patience with a stupid, clumsy offspring who sat hunched up, yelling for nourishment, and making his presence known to every cat within blocks.

The father cardinal did the training. He would fly to the

feeder, pick up a sunflower seed, peel it, take it to the fence, and slip it into Junior's beak. But before Junior could gulp it down, he would jerk it out again and fly back to the feeder, urging Junior to follow. However, Junior only yelled louder and made no effort to cooperate. After a number of futile trips, Father seemed to give up in despair and at last offered to let Junior *eat* the kernel. Instead of swallowing it, Junior promptly dropped it on the ground, and I could almost believe I saw a look of utter disgust on Father's face. He sat a moment gazing at his offspring, and then flew away, probably to tell Mother that her son was the dumbest member of the whole new, dumb generation, and hereafter, *she* could cope with him.

Once, during the season of feeding and training young, Lee and I saw an unusual, almost incredible incident. Some sparrows were on the feeding shelf, eating quietly, picking out small wild-bird seeds, when an adolescent cardinal arrived and tried to eat a fat sunflower seed. Finding he could not crack it, he set up a clamor for help, but his father was either occupied elsewhere or purposely ignoring him, for he did not come to his aid. Outraged, the young cardinal set up a squawking, screaming, and rasping which was almost unbearable even to the sparrows. Finally a female sparrow, who seemed to have had all she could stand of this din, opened a sunflower seed, hopped over, and thrust it into the noisy youngster's mouth. It was the only time we ever saw a bird of one species feed a bird of another species, except in the case of small cowbirds whose mothers lay eggs in other birds' nests, and whose young are often brought up by these foster parents.

We filled our feeder with crumbs, meat scraps, seeds, suet, and nuts—including doughnuts, for the birds loved them. During the winter months I often made bird candy for them, a concoction which provides them with warmth, nourishment, and pleasure. Here is the recipe:

Bird Candy

Large chunk of suet
Package of mixed wild-bird seed
Small jar of peanut butter

Cut the suet into large pieces, put into a skillet (preferably iron), and melt over burner adjusted to low heat, giving it *plenty* of time.

When the suet has become liquid, stir in the peanut butter and allow this to melt and blend. Then stir in as much wild-bird seed as the liquid will hold.

Pour into a shallow pan, cool, and cut into squares. These look like fudge and smell almost as appetizing. Store them in a cool place and serve on the feeder as needed. Giving birds this candy is much safer than giving them plain peanut butter, which is likely to choke and kill them.

Each time I put food on the shelf, I whistled in a certain way. The birds who lived around us learned to associate this whistle with food and to respond to it. After a while, I could open the window, whistle, and see them come flying down to me out of trees and sky. They would perch on branches near the window, unafraid, and watch me fill the shelf, but never consented to eat from my hand, though I think some of them would have done so, had I been able to spend more time in winning their trust.

My friend Marjorie, who lives in a wooded area, once lured some tufted titmice to her hand with nut meats. All four became so tame that they accompanied her, flying along beside her, when she went down to the country road for the mail, even when she went for a walk in the woods. When she called and held out a handful of black-walnut meats, one of them would flutter down and perch on her fingers while it ate. The smallest one ate from my hand in the same way once, and one of the most enchanting moments of my life was when this little bird, standing on my palm, lifted its head and sang its summertime song. I marveled at its size, for its little legs were no larger than the thinnest toothpicks.

As our birds grew accustomed to us, they became as demanding as spoiled children. Sometimes, when I had a difficult writing assignment and had worked until after midnight, I wanted to sleep late next morning, but the birds would not have it. They would perch in the trees or on the fence and call loudly for me to come and feed them. More than once a bluejay woke me, beating angrily against the windowpane with his wings.

One day a small fox squirrel came timidly to our feeder, and as soon as he spread the word, other fox squirrels began to come, some shy, some unafraid.

I once knew an editor of children's stories in an Eastern publishing firm who all but had a convulsion every time she received a manuscript in which birds or animals talked to each other. Indeed, I have met several "wildlife" and "outdoor" editors in Eastern publishing firms who knew no more about wildlife or the out-of-doors than I know about pretzel-weaving, and this woman headed the list. Her attitude was both uninformed and unobservant. For birds and animals *do* talk to one another, communicating the same needs and emotions which we communicate, and their vocabulary, like ours, possesses expressions of love, hate, kindness, comfort, sympathy, fear, wonder, indignation, anger, sorrow, suffering, and joy.

I have no doubt that the first little fox squirrel to find our feeder during that bitter winter hastened back to tell friends and relatives, "Just take the next street, go one block, turn to the left, look in the south yard at the red brick house, and you'll find all the nuts you can eat. . . ." True, this was uttered in squirrel talk instead of people talk, but the information was the same and the other squirrels promptly came to the right address.

Among them was a beautiful, tawny little creature who

took a great fancy to my husband, and since Lee loves animals, the attraction was mutual. He named the squirrel Charlie, but on closer acquaintance, discovered this to be an error in gender, and so changed it to Sharley.

Sharley was so tame it was obvious that we were not the first people she had met, though she evidently considered Lee the nicest of his kind. She would run to meet him whenever he appeared, follow at his heels like a puppy, and take food from his hand.

My friend Marjorie, and Carl her husband, shared our interest in wild pets, for living in a wooded region as they did, they had many of their own. Carl made a small shelter house for us to put in the lowest fork of an ash tree near our kitchen window. It was a small box, painted green for protective coloring, with a natural knothole from the woods for a doorway. The squirrels used it constantly, especially Sharley. On cold winter mornings she would wait in the little house until she heard a door or window open, then poke her head out to see if the snacks were ready. The other squirrels did the same, coming at various times throughout the day. We became accustomed to seeing a head pop out of the knothole whenever we appeared. The little animal always had an eager look, as if trying to ask, "Did you bring anything? Do we get anything?"

If one arrived while the house was occupied, however, there was what we called Instant Carnage. The occupant would spring out and chase the newcomer away with snarls and screams. I have seen this happen in the woods, too, when one squirrel *dared* approach another's den. Bill had assured me, though, that the most inhospitable would readily admit one that was ill, wounded, or being pursued by hunters.

Lee put ears of corn on the fence and wedged them into the forks of the trees, but soon found this would not do because the squirrels were carrying them away. He looked around for some way to anchor them and hit upon a unique and highly satisfactory plan. Most people have around the house at least one of those hazardous gadgets known as a "paper file"—the kind shaped like a large fishhook, which you fasten to the wall so you can jab down on it letters, bills, receipts, recipes, and often your thumb.

Lee nailed one of these to the ash tree and forced an ear of corn down upon it, the hook penetrating the cob. This held the corn so firmly that the most determined squirrel could not remove it and had to be content with sharing it.

Sharley used to climb the tree, sit down on the ear of corn, and wrap her back legs around it, an ungainly pose and a hilarious sight. This, however, left her "arms and hands" free to deal with the kernels. Like all other squirrels, she ate only the heart of each grain, dropping the rest on the ground, a careless habit which pleases birds and hunters equally, since it feeds the birds and guides the hunters. Those who understand the woods can always follow a squirrel's movements by reading the "sign" he has left behind, mutilated grains of corn by a fence, acorn tops tossed under a tree, walnuts thoroughly bitten and dropped to the ground. Sharley left plenty of "sign" beneath the ash tree, and the birds gathered there to feast upon it, just as they do in the wilds. I loved to watch her eat, for she held her food in her little hands like a child. (And a squirrel *does* have hands—four fingers and a tiny stub of a thumb.)

Nearly all wild animals have a burning curiosity and many have lost their lives because of it. Sharley was very curious about people and loved to observe them. There was an elm tree in front of our house, shading the sidewalk, and Sharley spent many happy afternoons in it. Stretched flat on a low branch, when the day was sunny and not too cold, she would lie perfectly still and watch people going up and down the street just beneath her, her eyes following them with intense interest.

Spring came and the weather grew warm. Some of the

squirrels continued to visit our shelter house and feeder, but I noticed that they were nibbling green leaves and shoots now, and feasting on the flowerlets of the redbud tree. Some had vanished, probably to seek mates, for such sentimental journeys are a part of their nature. Bill believed that the mating season lasted from late December until mid-July, with May and June the most important months.

One summer morning I saw a new squirrel on the feeder, a stranger and a "traveler" (migrant), new to our community. His coloring was unlike our squirrels, and his tail was thin and scrubby from being dragged through miles of woodlands.

This particular traveler looked like a Squirrel Town hoodlum. He was extremely light for a fox squirrel, almost silvery, and had black markings which included an astonishing black mask across his eyes. You felt that if he were a human, he'd wear a tight black sweater and cap and have a cigarette hanging from his lower lip. He ate a hearty meal, skipped town, and we never saw him again.

Not long afterward, I glanced out of the living-room window one afternoon and saw Sharley coming down the trunk of a large tree which shaded the street near our house. It had been raining earlier and the ground was wet. While I watched, Sharley began to take damp leaves in her mouth and carry them up into the tree. She made innumerable trips, each time taking as many leaves as she could carry.

The next day she did not come to the feeder, nor the next, nor the next. Still, we were not concerned, for she had attracted the attention and interest of other people in our block and scampered all over the neighborhood begging nuts and sunflower seeds. However, when a week had gone by and she did not appear, we began to worry about her. There was a great deal of traffic on our street, and on several occasions Lee had picked up and buried a furry little body run down by a car, though he found no trace of Sharley. We knew, too, that squirrels are always disappearing and reappearing, habits related to food and mating. Every morning Lee went out and called hopefully, but no little face popped out of the knothole and no little pet came running to his outstretched hand.

Weeks passed. One day in late summer we were coming down the street when a fox squirrel, ragged, thin, disheveled, and incredibly dirty ran down the elm tree, sat up in front of Lee, and looked at him beseechingly. I did not recognize her at all, and was surprised when he said, "*Sharley!* Is it really *you?*"

Immediately she ran to him and began following at his heels. He led her around the house, brought nuts and fruit for her, and fed her by hand, all the while talking to her and petting her as if she were a puppy.

"*Where* have you been?" I heard him ask.

"Can't you see?" I answered. "She's nursing young."

This explained her long absence. Evidently she had been in her den with babies for weeks, for she was terribly gaunt and her beautiful coat was dull and matted, as if they had mussed and soiled her fur. She ate hungrily from Lee's hand and he said, in some concern, "Listen to the queer noises she's making. . . ."

I listened. The sounds came from deep in her throat and were like "*Mm . . . mm . . . mm . . . mm.*" We didn't know then that this is a fox squirrel's expression of love.

When she finished eating, she looked pleased and refreshed. Lee gave her small head a final pat and she scampered away, back to her nest and her babies. We never saw her again.

Four or five days passed and still she didn't return. Little is known about the ways of fox squirrels, but it was Bill's belief that the mother remains in the nest until the little ones are old enough to open their eyes, nursing them, caring for them, keeping them warm. During this time, she becomes very thin. How she eats is not known, perhaps from some store in her den. After the babies open their eyes, she comes out to forage in the woods again, to eat green things, drink from a creek possibly, find wild fruits and berries. When the babies are weaned, she brings them outside the den and begins to train them in caution, foraging, traveling in the trees, hiding and fleeing from danger.

Males and females live together, he thought, until the young were born. Then the male left, but stayed close to the family if he was a native of the vicinity. If the mother was killed during the nursing period, he went into the nest and destroyed the babies. (At least, he said, that was what some people *claimed*, though none of them seemed to have witnessed it.)

There is an old hunter's tale which says that if the mother does not protect her young constantly and savagely, the father will enter the nest and castrate all the males. Motive: jealousy. I had heard this story many times, but when I discussed it with Bill, he dismissed it as folklore. Once in a while he shot a male that appeared to have been castrated, but he thought this was due to some accident in the woods. Animals are always getting hurt, often in fights for their lives. Also, there are bodily changes in the male after the mating season is over which give him the appearance of having been castrated, probably the real basis for the story.

Sharley's babies, we thought, must be nearly old enough to come out of the nest, or she would not have left them. Something must have happened to her; she was hurt or had been killed. Lee went out and searched the streets, but found no sign of her tawny little body.

The next morning I kept hearing a strange cry near the house. It sounded like a bluejay, yet I knew it *wasn't* a bluejay. It sounded like a bird, but what bird ever possessed so shrill, agonized, and penetrating a call? I asked Lee, "Did you notice any unusual birds around the feeder? I keep hearing something very strange. . . ."

He went outside to look and in a few moments returned, bringing, not a bird, but a baby squirrel. It was so little its eyes were scarcely open, and though its tail and body were covered with soft fine fur, it was barely able to sit up, and its ears were still flat against its head. It clung to Lee's chest, its little arms outflung, its little hands clutching the fabric of his shirt.

"Don't worry, little fellow," said Lee, soothingly. "We'll take care of you."

The baby whimpered and clung to him. At that moment, a whole new life began for this furry foundling—and for us.

IV Jamie, our daughter, hastened to the ten-cent store and brought back some rubber-tipped nursing bottles, doll size, while I mixed a formula for the animal. I combined milk and corn syrup, as for a baby, and because I had heard old hunters say that the milk of mother squirrels has a nut-like flavor, I added the tiniest bit of peanut butter.

When this mixture was warm and properly tested on the wrist, we gave the bottle to the baby squirrel. He clutched it with both hands and drank so desperately that we knew he was almost starved.

While he drank, we examined him carefully. Perhaps he was one of Sharley's litter, we said, even though he did not resemble her in the least. He was much grayer than she; indeed he was almost silvery, and had striking black markings which included the trace of a black mask across his eyes.

When I looked at him, I remembered the strange squirrel I had seen at the feeder in early summer, sometime in May, and felt sure that he was this baby's father. Plainly this evil stranger had seduced our innocent Sharley, and then abandoned her, for he had never been seen again and, by now, was probably miles away, back in his home territory.

We put the baby squirrel in a box lined with an old towel where he cried in a lonely, desolate way, missing the warmth and companionship of the nest. When he refused to be comforted, we devised a sort of "mother substitute" for him. I brought a pot holder, the kind shaped like a glove, and into this Lee slipped the smallest possible light bulb, connecting it to an outlet above the box. When the glove became warm, the little squirrel cuddled up to it and was content. We covered him with what we later came to call "squirrel blankets"—pieces of old terry towels, each about ten inches square.

Now we began to worry about the rest of the babies, and I tried to remember what I had heard about the size and nature of squirrel litters years ago. On crisp fall days, after a morning's hunting, Bill and his cronies sometimes sat around the little stove in the incredible kitchen and drank coffee and talked about the woods and its wildlife. Old hunters are often real authorities on wildlife, though how a hunter can love animals and still destroy them is a paradox I will never understand.

Many times I would sit on the steps, cleaning and polishing my rifle, and listen fascinated to their stories, observations, and discussions. I remembered hearing them agree that the average squirrel litter is three. One man said he had seen a litter of six. Another said he had come to believe that the older the mother, the larger the litter, though none had ever seen more than six, nor less than two. The mothers, they thought, mated twice a year, maybe three times, depending upon the previous winter. If it had been a hard winter when the food was scarce and the snow had stayed on longer than usual, the squirrels would be half-starved, weak, and perhaps ill. In such years they did not mate as early as usual and therefore had fewer little ones. The men were in agreement, however, that there are squirrels born every month between December and August in normal years, especially if the mast is heavy. (They were always talking about "the mast," the nut crop, because a good mast meant good hunting.) Nobody knew the period of gestation for a squirrel, but they reckoned six weeks was about right.

Sharley was young, and if their theories were correct, she had given birth to three babies, probably. But where were the other two, and where did Sharley live? Was her nest in the elm tree where I had seen her carrying the damp leaves? It should have occurred to me then that she might be preparing it for young. Wherever she lived, two little squirrels were probably dying of exposure and starvation at this moment.

Sometimes a curious baby, exploring the world for the first time, falls from his home tree and wanders away, but we did not think this true of our foundling. We thought he had emerged in a desperate attempt to seek his mother and food. There seemed no doubt now that Sharley was dead.

Lee went out and examined all the trees near our house, but could find no outdoor nest and no opening which looked like a den. However, we knew that such dens were usually very high, well hidden by leaves, and extremely hard to find. In the woods there are ways of locating squirrel dens by scent, but not in town, probably because den trees in the woods are used by many squirrels for many years and the scent is stronger. Too, the dampness of the woods seems to make it more apparent.

A squirrel may build her nest in a hollow vacated by an owl, a raccoon, or some other creature of the wilds. She likes to use a flicker hole as an entrance because it is well made and does not have to be gnawed out again later, for flickers build in dead trees and the edges of the holes do not grow together as in live trees. Sharley had obviously built her den in a live tree, and we felt that her nest would be found deep inside, possibly in a hole made by storm damage. Summer nests built outside in a tree fork are not so common in town as in the woods.

Lee hunted all afternoon, inspecting all the trees in the neighborhood, but saw no more baby squirrels, nor did he hear any more distress calls. About sunset, however, he noticed something orange-bright high up in the elm tree. It was a baby squirrel peeping out of a hole and it was as tawny as Sharley, so tawny that the setting sun made its fur as bright as flame.

The hole was so high we couldn't possibly reach it, so we telephoned Don McBride, who heads our park department and has personally rescued and brought up some of the animals in our park zoo. By the time we reached him it was almost dark, too late to get the little squirrels down, he thought, so we had to wait until morning.

Early next day he and one of his assistants came with a long ladder, but it wouldn't reach after all, so we called the fire department. They said they would be glad to join in the rescue if the police would reroute traffic for them, as they would need to block the street with their truck. So we called the police. In a few moments there was an officer on the corner directing traffic, a ladder being raised from the fire truck, and Mr. McBride going up into the tree with leather gloves on his hands and a basket on his arm. At that moment I was proud of living in a town where people would go to all this trouble to aid two forsaken baby squirrels.

When Mr. McBride came down again, he held out my basket and said, "Two of them . . . but I'm afraid we're too late. They're nearly gone."

The den was so deeply hidden that he had to chop away part of a limb to reach it. He had lifted the babies into the basket, nest and all. The nest was made of leaves, blossoms, herbs, and grass, and smelled like hay and mint. The little squirrels were sprawled on their faces, barely breathing. We hurried them into the house through a crowd of people who had gathered to see what was going on, ignoring remarks like, "I'd sure like to have one of them squirrels, I'd sure pay well for it," and "For heaven's sake, I thought it was something *important!*"

We now had the full litter, three babies, two males and a female. Later my sister-in-law suggested that we name them Shadrach, Meshach, and Abednego "because they had been through so much," and the first one was always called Shad. The tawny little female became Mimi. Abednego was too cumbersome a name for such a tiny little fellow and when later (during his adolescence) he took to loud complaints, we called him Groany.

Though of the same litter, they appeared to be about a month apart in size and development. Shad was the largest, Mimi was middle-size, and Groany was extremely small. But Groany had a huge appetite, snatched his bottle with both hands, and drank hard and fast. We could not get it away from him. He was a soft brown color with a snow-white tummy and four white feet, like small white socks. Mimi, the little flame-colored one, looked most like Sharley. She was almost dead, unable to open her eyes or lift her head. Jamie fed her with a medicine dropper, and after a day or so she seemed to regain her strength and went happily into the box with Shad. They cuddled together as fondly as puppies.

Each of us had a squirrel to bring up. Lee had already adopted Shad, Jamie was responsible for Mimi, and I chose Groany because he was the weakest and the most pitiful. He was too frail to be handled much or to be put with the others. I wrapped him in warm "blankets" when he had finished his milk and laid him in a box by himself. Several times that night I got up to look at him, worried because he was breathing heavily and with difficulty. Perhaps there was something else wrong with him besides weakness and shock; perhaps he had been injured. Very carefully I opened his blankets to examine him and was horrified and revolted by my discovery. Fly maggots!

These hideous creatures, the larvae of the flesh fly, will devour living tissue. They emerge from eggs laid by the flies and attack the eyes, wounds, and tender portions of helpless animals, eating them alive. There were several in Groany's left eye, burrowing under the eyeball.

I went to the kitchen and made camomile tea, a back-country remedy sometimes used as a repellent. I then immobilized Groany by wrapping him gently but firmly in one of the blankets, and while Lee held him, dropped tea into his eye with a medicine dropper. It caused no pain but did bring the fly maggots to the surface. Quickly, and without hurting the baby animal, I snatched them out with my eyebrow tweezers.

Examining Groany further I found that the two stronger squirrels, seeking their mother and desperate with hunger, had gnawed his leg until the tendon was exposed. With mild soapsuds in a small syringe, we flushed out the three fly maggots we found there and treated the wound with a sulfa tablet dissolved in water.

One or two people suggested, "Why don't you just put the poor little thing out of his misery?" But Groany was so helpless and clung to me so trustingly that I could not bear to have him destroyed. I went on treating and feeding him. He ate greedily, grew stronger, and his leg healed nicely.

At first we fed these starved babies every three hours. At feeding time each of us would pick up our squirrel, wrap it cosily in a blanket, sit down, and feed it. They grasped the doll bottles tightly in their little hands and refused to let go until the last drop had vanished.

Since Groany was so small and frail, we did not put him in the box with the others for some time, afraid they might hurt him. He became very dependent upon me, would cry plaintively when he wanted me, and showed a strong desire to spend all his time at my shoulder. He would cling to me desperately, fight against being taken from me, with an astonishing show of temper, and seemed frightened when separated from me. Lee said, "If you don't put him with the others, you're going to have a very neurotic child."

The next day I laid him in their box and they ran to him as though delighted to see him. Then suddenly Shad threw him down and held him. I was going to his rescue when I saw the reason for this action. Shad was licking his injured eye. Carefully and very tenderly, he licked it every day, as did Mimi. In no time at all it had healed, though the fly maggots had injured it irreparably. The eyeball was intact and looked perfectly all right, but the sight of that eye was gone.

Healing an eye by licking it with the tongue is done, not only by animals, but by primitive peoples and certain other groups. It is a very ancient gypsy remedy and many a gypsy mother has endured this unpleasant experience in order to heal her child. As for camomile tea, it has been used for generations in back-country Indiana for the treating of sore and inflamed eyes due to external causes. Camomile (sometimes called mayweed) grows wild in Indiana, blooming in meadows, fields, and along roadsides. Pioneers gathered it, dried it, and brewed an aromatic tea from its fragrant blossoms. Camomile tea was valued as a pleasing drink, a tonic, a rinse that made hair soft and shining, and a soothing wash for the eyes. Today it may be purchased (cleaned and dried and boxed) at any place which sells crude drugs. I have used it in my eyes all my life, and with it have healed the eyes of my sister and my dog. For some reason its herbal odor, quite pleasing to humans, seems to repel certain parasites, and was certainly effective in helping me to locate and eradicate the fly maggots.

Since young squirrels begin to come out of the nest and forage on the ground when they are about three months old, we decided ours were less than that, possibly eight or nine weeks. We found them in August and, basing our calculations upon the appearance of the persuasive traveler in May, believed they had been born in June. True, their eyes were open and they had all their baby fur (though their tails were still skimpy) but only Shad could sit up.

Once or twice I have found a newborn squirrel in the woods, dead, but I had never seen one alive. Babies do not often fall from a den, but are sometimes blown out of summer nests during heavy storms. Marjorie rescued one that was less than a week old, after hearing its call of acute distress echoing through the woods around her home.

Like me, Marjorie had read of this call but had never heard it and was unable to identify it. Like me, she thought it the cry of a strange bird. She first heard it about nine in the morning on a hot August day and immediately went into the woods to investigate, feeling that some wild creature was in trouble. All day the call sounded through the woods, again and again, while Marjorie searched the trees with field glasses, expecting to see a strange or injured bird.

About five o'clock in the afternoon her mother, who was visiting her at the time, went into the woods to aid in the search and, led by the piercing cry, discovered the little animal at the base of an oak tree on a pile of leaves. Newborn squirrels are anything but handsome, and neither she nor Marjorie knew what they had found.

Such babies are about the size of a thumb, as pink and as hairless. The heads seem abnormally large, the eyes are closed, and the little one is helpless and blind. They are said to weigh only about half an ounce.

Marjorie and her mother rescued the foundling and, by the process of elimination, decided it *must* be a squirrel, since it bore no resemblance to any of the other animals in the woods. They took it to the house, where Marjorie wrapped it warmly in a piece of terry cloth and fed it diluted milk from a doll bottle.

The baby squirrel seemed to thrive. It ate heartily, slept contentedly, and uttered its wild, desperate cry no more. In a few days, Marjorie observed a light fuzz of hair on the back of its head and between its shoulders. At this point a squirrel is about a week old and, if it is healthy, weighs about an ounce. In five weeks it had fur all over its body, even on the underneath part of its tail, which is the last to grow. Contrary to what one might expect, the fur of a baby squirrel is not fine or soft, but rather coarse and harsh to the touch.

Marjorie had begun to think its eyes would never open and was worried because its little belly became grossly distended after every meal. She therefore went to consult Claude, a veteran squirrel hunter now past seventy who had been a friend of Bill.

Like Bill, Claude knew a lot about wildlife. He told her not to worry, the baby's eyes would open by the time it was six weeks old, which they did. He advised her *not* to dilute its milk, but to use it whole, no matter what she had read in a book.

"Books know damn little about squirrels," he said dryly.

Marjorie followed his advice and the baby no longer suffered distention. Also, she added a small amount of corn syrup to the milk in order to keep the little one's bowels normally active. The squirrel was a beautiful little female, and Marjorie named her Patsy.

Soon after Patsy's eyes were open, she began to play, to move around, and to practice sitting up. She developed rapidly, adored Marjorie, would eat from her hand and ride around on her shoulder. Marjorie became extremely fond of this cute and affectionate little pet and loved to watch her merry antics, but was haunted by the feeling that she was wronging her by keeping her in the house instead of letting her return to the woods.

Bill told me once, "If you get them before their mothers have taught them, you'd better *keep* them. Because if their mothers have never taught them, they'll never really learn to look after themselves"—something I now believe to be true. And it was his conviction that if their mothers *had* taught them, they could never really be tamed. Of course a squirrel raised in captivity might possibly find a mate, he said, from which to learn caution and survival. But often, before this can happen, his friendly curiosity will lead him to approach an animal or person that will harm or kill him.

Marjorie consulted a naturalist who told her it would be safe to release the little squirrel after it was three months old, in early November. Sometimes we are still having Indian summer in November, a warm and langorous season which the wild things seem to love. Marjorie decided to release Patsy then, so she could become accustomed to the woods and make a home for herself before winter came.

In preparation for this step Carl, Marjorie's husband, built a little house which they put in the kitchen, and Patsy slept in it every night. Then Carl moved the house to a tree outside the kitchen window and Patsy slept there. Early each morning, however, she would arrive at the house and come in through the window to get her breakfast—a piece of apple, a few sunflower seeds, some nut meats. Sometimes she drank water served in an ashtray, but not always, as squirrels rarely drink. When she had finished eating, Marjorie took her back to the woods, where she played in the trees. Then one day she was gone and did not return. Winter passed and spring came, but there was no sign of Patsy.

During the time Patsy was growing up, Marjorie would leave her in the care of the hunter, Claude, and his wife whenever she and Carl had to be away. Claude and his wife became very fond of her, as did Claude's sister, Mrs. Brians, who petted the little squirrel and made much of her.

The Brians family lived on the other side of town, a good seven or eight miles from Marjorie's home. One day when Mrs. Brians went out to sweep the back steps, a squirrel came running up and tried to go into the house with her. Mrs. Brians was frightened, because a wild animal that shows no fear and tries to mingle with people or domestic herds may be rabid. She drove it away, but watched it carefully and saw that it was living in a nearby tree, that it seemed to behave quite normally and did not appear to be ill.

Soon afterward, she found it in her garage, pilfering walnuts from a bag stored there, and observed that for all its trying, the little squirrel could not open a nut. This made her suspect that the animal had been raised in captivity. She looked at it more closely and wondered if it could be Patsy, if Patsy had recognized her and followed her for that reason. (This would not surprise anyone who is well acquainted with the ways of squirrels. Old hunters tell many true stories about the affection and remembrance of squirrels for people who have raised or cared for them.)

Mrs. Brians telephoned Marjorie and asked if Patsy had run away. Marjorie explained that her pet had disappeared from the woods, but she did not believe Patsy could travel seven or eight miles through town streets and National Road traffic without coming to harm. However, she went to see for herself, and called Patsy the way she had always called her. The little squirrel came flying from a tree, leaped to Marjorie's shoulder, and answered with the "*Mm . . . mm . . . mm . . . mm*" that is love talk.

She was living in a big maple and had obviously found a mate, for they could see that she was carrying young. Sadly, but feeling that it was best for the little squirrel, Marjorie decided against taking her home again, a decision she has always regretted, for Patsy would gladly have gone with her.

Patsy remained in the maple tree, petted and fed by Mrs. Brians. It was because she was carrying young, however, that she could not run fast enough to get away when, a little later, a dog caught her and killed her.

It was less than a year since Marjorie had found her in the woods, and she must have mated during her first breeding season, when she was about ten months old.

Soon after we rescued our own little squirrels, the newspaper published a story about them. That night a little old man came to the house and told us what had happened to Sharley. He said he lived down the street, had fed her and petted her many times. One morning he had seen her killed by a truck, had gathered up her crushed little body and buried it in his garden. His eyes filled with tears as he told us about it.

He was a pensioner almost eighty years old who lived all alone. Every day he and two equally elderly cronies, also pensioners, went to sit in the sun in the little park where Sharley sometimes played. They had made a game of feeding her, hiding nuts in their pockets and watching her hunt them out. Now she was gone.

The next day he came back, bringing the second member of their trio. This man told me he had owned a pet squirrel when he was a boy. He and his brothers had gone hunting one day, and were on their way home when their squirrel-dog began to bark furiously. They went over to see what he wanted, and found him standing guard over a baby squirrel that had evidently fallen from a nest.

The dog had been trained to kill squirrels and usually dispatched them on sight, but he seemed to know that *this* one was a baby, lost and starving, and wanted them to help it. They took it home, raised it, loved it dearly.

"And," said the old man solemnly, "I've never shot another one to this day."

On another evening the two visitors returned bringing the third old man, explaining in earnest tones, "He knew her well." I was sorry for them, deprived of the pet they had loved, that had brought so much pleasure to their lonely lives. They looked at her babies and were delighted with them, but the last little old man wept openly to think they would see her no more.

After reading the newspaper story, several people wrote to tell me about squirrels they had owned and raised, and perfect strangers came to the door, asking to see them. Several were what we termed "reformed hunters."

One man told how he had shot a small squirrel that was feeding in a hickory tree, intent upon opening a nut. When the bullet struck, the squirrel dropped the nut and clapped its tiny hands over its ears. He picked it up and saw that even in death, its hands were holding its bleeding little head.

"I sat there a long time," he said. "Then I promised it that I'd never shoot another one . . . and I never did."

Thinking about it, he wondered why he had ever wanted to shoot squirrels at all. They were too small to make a good meal, and not a bit easy to clean.

"In pioneer days it was different. But today, with every kind of meat, with freezers and all . . ." He shook his head. "Of course, some people claim they're destructive, but I don't believe they do any real harm."

Conservationists, too, are of this opinion. True, squirrels love growing things, pilfer a few ears of corn from the fields, steal bites from pears, apples, and tomatoes, but the amount they eat is negligible. The real danger, conservationists say, is one of overpopulation, which would mean hunger and suffering for all.

Another man confessed that his hunting days had ended on a bright autumn morning when he shot a tawny little female out of the top of a beech tree.

"I could see her up there playing," he said. "I guess it was such a beautiful day and she was so glad to be alive that she forgot to watch. As I hit her she fell to the ground, but she wasn't quite dead, and when I leaned over her, she looked up at me and sobbed. I . . . I just couldn't get over it. I buried her there in the woods, and went home and put my squirrel gun away, and never picked it up again."

One afternoon there was a knock at the door and I opened it to see standing there a grizzled man who resembled a movie version of a Kentucky mountaineer. As a matter of fact, he *wasn't* long out of the Kentucky mountains, and looked so rough that I was half afraid of him.

"This-here the place whar the squirrels is?"

I said yes and he added politely, "Mand if I tyke a look at the laytle varmints?"

I said no and he came in and stood by their box and looked at them for a long time. Finally, he reached out a dirty, calloused hand and stroked Mimi's bright fur. I was astonished to see that his eyes had grown red and moist.

"I had me a squirrel oncet," he said, in a low voice. "Hit dad . . . and I crad fer two year." Then he said, "Mybee some tam I'll fand me another one," and on this hopeful note, he went away.

We were fascinated by our baby squirrels and the amazing, unbelievable things they did. When we petted them, they purred like kittens, or made a soft burbling sound like a percolator. They played hide and seek, a game that is natural to them, and which I have watched wild squirrels play for hours in the woods. They alternated between sharp quarrels over food, and tender moments during which they would nuzzle or gently scratch one another. Sometimes one would steal the other's food and run with it, while the robbed one screamed loudly and furiously. They romped like children and tumbled like kittens, playing. They curled up together in their box when sleeping, an indefinable mass of fur, feet, and ears. This sight (it is said) gave us the pioneer Indiana expression still used in some back-country areas, "You couldn't tell heads from tails."

At night we were always peeping into their box and calling each other to come and look *quick!* There they lay, the three of them, sleeping spoon-fashion, one curled against the back of the other. Or, more often, they slept with their arms around each other, like children. Mimi was very motherly, and seemed to look after the others. Sometimes she would sleep on her back, with an arm around each of them, an engaging sight scarcely to be believed.

On hot nights we lined their box with cleansing tissue instead of terry blankets, as this was cooler for them. Accustomed to the darkness of the nest, they disliked having light in the room when they were trying to sleep.

One night Lee went out to look at them and came back saying, "Now, I know you won't believe this . . . but when I turned on the light to get a drink, a little hand came out and snatched up a piece of tissue. It was Mimi, and she pulled it over her eyes to keep the light out."

I had to admit that this sounded far-fetched, but we soon grew accustomed to the almost-human things they did, and came to accept them as perfectly natural. However, they made me remember something I had not thought about in years.

Once I had said, "Bill, don't you think animals are a lot like humans?"

"Nope," he answered, "it's the other way around. Humans is a lot like animals."

V

Shad and Mimi soon learned that they could jump out of their box and back in again, a delightful game. They kept at it all day, like furry little jumping jacks, but Groany was afraid to jump or play. When I tried to put him down on the floor with them, he cried pitifully and clung to my shoulder, so frightened that his little heart beat violently.

One morning I put their box on a table, thinking this would keep them in it for a while, but they jumped out anyway. Shad sat awhile, considering the matter thoughtfully. He seemed to calculate his moves, jumped first to a chair, then to a stool, and last to the floor. Mimi, however, was too impatient, or perhaps too feminine, for such deliberation. She leaped right out in mid-air and had several falls. We did not worry about her, however, for squirrels spend a good part of their lives airborne, and can easily leap as far as forty feet without injury or fear. A squirrel pursued by a hunter and desperate to escape may leap from a tree seventy feet high and land on the ground running. The spread of his furry legs and tail provide him with a sort of swift parachute descent.

Eventually I coaxed Groany to join the others on the floor, but he could not run as they did. His leg seemed to bother him still, and he paddled about in an awkward, unnatural way.

Mimi saw this and immediately took him in hand and taught him to run. She would run ahead of him a little way, hop, skip, then wait for him to catch up. He paddled after her as awkwardly as ever. Then she would turn back and run again, showing him how it was done. They appeared to be communicating with sounds I could not hear. Every time she looked around, with her mouth moving, he tried to correct his gait. Soon he was running with her.

Carl sent us a roomy cage for them, which Shad and Mimi climbed merrily, but Groany was afraid to try. With motherly tenderness, Mimi turned back to teach him and finally, timidly and awkwardly, he followed her. Later he became the best of the three at climbing, and would shinny up a round chrome table leg, then slide down with his arms around it, like a veteran fireman.

As they were permitted to explore the house, Shad and Mimi learned to run up one of the draperies in the den, but when I put Groany on it he was stricken with terror, and his whole little body shook with the force of his heartbeat. I lifted him back to my shoulder and said to him, half whispering, "Now, now . . . nothing is going to hurt you . . ." and found that he relaxed at once and was content. From that day forward, he was comforted and reassured if I spoke to him in this way. Whenever he was afraid, he would huddle against my shoulder and lift his head to my lips and wait, wanting me to whisper to him.

After a while, he learned to play on the back stairs with Mimi, and the two of them would scamper up and down the steps with great glee. Shad, however, was too intelligent for such primitive methods, and too mature for such childish antics. After thinking the matter over, he went up and down on the rail and never once bothered with the steps.

It was not necessary to housebreak them. All squirrels are naturally "housebroken" and, even in the woods, will not void in their nests, but will seek dry leaves on the ground or in some sheltered spot. In captivity they find a newspaper just as satisfactory. Their droppings (mostly in the morning) are like small, dry, morning-glory seeds, odorless and inoffensive. A small odorless puddle, usually morning and evening, completes the process. Actually, squirrels are among the cleanest of pets, for their coats are self-cleansing, like the coat of a dachshund, and they do not require baths. When we first acquired our pets, however, they seemed somewhat dusty and soiled from weeks in the nest, so after deciding that they were innocent of fleas, we wiped them clean with pieces of cotton dipped in warm camomile tea and wrung out, being careful not to get them really wet. If they have any odor in captivity, it is the faint odor of new-mown hay. In the wilds, however, they have a gamy smell.

Their ears were still flat against their heads. Bill once told me that mother squirrels lick the ears of their young in order to make them stand upright. We stroked their ears with a soft damp cloth dipped in warm water and wrung out, and soon they stayed erect.

Shad was the first to learn to sit upright and eat in the normal pose of a feeding squirrel. Mimi tried, immediately lost her balance, and fell over backward, a hilarious though pathetic sight. Not at all dismayed, she picked up her bottle, propped herself up in one corner of the cage, and finished her lunch there. Groany still ate lying down.

About this time they began to talk to each other in sounds we could hear, saying, "*Cr-onk, crrrrrrr-onk,*" as they played or rested, a sound much like a mother hen talking to her chicks. They greeted us each morning with affectionate grunting noises, "*Mm . . . mm . . . mm . . . mm.*" Now they not only washed, but combed their heads (forward) with their claws.

They played together and they played alone. Each would amuse himself for a long time, leaping, jumping, twisting, turning, running back and forth, bucking like a bronco, jumping stiff-legged into the air. They chased each other, tumbling and squalling. They seemed to call to each other repeatedly, looking around, their mouths moving, but at such times I could hear no sound. In the midst of their wildest games, they might collapse on the floor and take a short rest or a brief nap, then leap up and resume their play where they had left off. Once, while leaping happily across the floor, Groany suddenly tumbled down on his back and lay rigid, his four little feet in the air. I thought he had had some sort of an attack and died, but he was only napping. Instant Sleep, we called it, and never saw anything like it.

Visitors were always telling us, "Yes, they're cute while they're little, but you can't really tame them, they're too wild. When they're older, they'll get mean and turn on you."

We decided to bring up our little pets like kittens or puppies, with affectionate care, nourishing food, gentle training, and *see!*

We began to train them in social behavior. When, in play, one of them nipped our fingers too sharply, we would flip him on the nose and say, "Too hard!" They learned this rebuke as a puppy might learn it, and bit more gently after that.

There was an old man in the neighborhood—who was *not* named Mr. Dubbs, but who will be called that in these pages. Mr. Dubbs had once raised a litter of squirrels and he came by nearly every day to give me some more advice at the top of his voice. Mr. Dubbs was no hunter, no naturalist, no woodsman, not even a wildlife fancier, but he thought he knew all there was to know about squirrels and, in retrospect, I must say that he knew a good deal. Some of his statements, however, were simply too ridiculous to be endured. For instance, he insisted that squirrels knock on windows to attract attention, and on doors to be admitted.

"Jest like other folks," he informed me. "No diff-rence."

One day he said, "You think Groany is yours? Ha! Ha! *You* can't divide up squirrels like they was apples. Squirrels has got minds of their own, and as soon as they're old enough to think about it, *they'll* pick out who they want to belong to, and *you* won't have nothing to say about it!

"And you'd better be mighty careful how you talk to 'em because they got tender feelings, *awful* tender feelings. Mark my words, if you ever do anything to hurt a squirrel's pride, he'll never speak to you again, come hell or high water . . . *never!*"

I must admit that I thought Mr. Dubbs was dotty and did not believe a word he said, but the time came when I had to revise my opinion completely.

By late September we had the squirrels long enough to note the differences in their character traits, mental traits, and personalities. Shad still looked a month older than Mimi, and Mimi still looked a month older than Groany. Shad and Mimi could now sit up as straight as any squirrel in the woods, and Groany was doing his best. When he fell over backward, however, he was terrified and would scramble up and come running to me for comfort. I would cuddle him against my shoulder and whisper to him, things like, "You can do it . . . of course you can do it . . . nothing's going to hurt you . . . ," which seemed to console him immensely. Then I would put him back on the floor, and after a while he would try again, and be a little less terrified each time he fell.

We were astonished to find these little animals so sensitive, especially Shad. If we scolded him he would creep, as though brokenhearted, to a far corner of the cage and sit there, hanging his head. Groany, too, was easily hurt, but Mimi was a brazen little baggage who paid no attention to scoldings, *unless* they came from Lee. She would defy me, even chatter at me with unmistakable insolence, and obeyed me only when I rapped her plump posterior with a six-inch ruler.

Shad was highly affectionate, intelligent, trusting, and tender of heart. He was now light gray in color, and his black markings seemed even more pronounced. All the way up his stomach he had a straight, but somewhat ragged black line that looked for all the world like a zipper. When he was about three months old, a bluejay came screaming to the window. Shad rose up with instinctive indignation, barked loudly, and sat down with a thud, staring in amazement at his own unexpected talents.

Mimi was the prettiest squirrel I have ever seen, and looked far more like a stuffed toy than a living animal. For one thing, her color was an incredible gold-red, and while many squirrels are rather long and thin, Mimi was short and cute and plump. She was light and graceful in her movements, and tripped about as daintily as a ballet dancer, for which reason she was given nicknames like Prancy, Dancy, and Fancy. One of her favorite pastimes was parading up and down the top of the double dresser, watching her reflection in the wide mirror. Whatever she thought this reflection might be, she was smart enough to peep behind the mirror, trying to find it.

Groany still wore his white "baby socks" and his little white vest. Day and night, he groomed himself, combing, scrubbing, drying, smoothing every hair, arranging his tail so that it was thick and fluffy. He had begun to grow manly whiskers and took very good care of them, keeping them in perfect order. He loved to romp and play, was obedient, affectionate, and good, but still very timid and very tiny.

The three squirrels romped around the house during the day and slept in their cage at night. In the mornings they woke early, but sat for an hour or two in a stupor from which nothing could rouse them. It was very strange—something I had never seen and have never understood.

Once really awake, they stretched long and luxuriously, yawned widely, and then set up a terrific clamor for their bottles.

We noticed, when we picked them up to be fed or petted, that their feet were either very hot or very cold, depending upon whether they had been in their bed or on the floor, and could change temperature instantly. Also, at this point in their lives, their feet exuded an invisible substance, possibly oil, which we were never able to identify, but which left, on polished surfaces, prints that were almost impossible to erase, and which could remove a chrome finish. As they grew older, however, this substance seemed to disappear, as we no longer found traces of it where they had walked or run.

Also as they grew older, the pink soles of their feet turned black and their little white teeth became red. In fact, a mature squirrel's teeth are so bright that their mouths may appear to be bleeding.

Wild animals in captivity seem to lose or forget, at least temporarily, some of the instincts they share in the woods. When our pets were very little, the rustle of paper seemed to be associated in their minds with danger, for the rustle of paper sounds like approaching footsteps upon dead leaves, and their mother may have taught them in the nest to beware of this sound. Hearing it, they would freeze, then slip into their blankets so silently that they seemed to "melt" out of sight. For a long time, they would remain hidden, as still as little mice.

In time, however, they ceased to associate this with danger and instead, associated it with food, since they often heard the rustle of paper bags just before we fed them. After a while, they would come running like children to look in the bags and see what we had brought.

Suddenly one morning Shad put down his bottle and never touched it again. Nothing could persuade him to drink from it. About a week later Mimi did the same thing, and soon afterward Groany joined them. *That quick*, they were weaned!

Nobody seemed to know just what to feed them at this point, and I could find no books to help me. The veterinarian told me not much was known about their nutrition, and said it was during the period of transition from liquid to solid food that most of these little pets died. I consulted a naturalist, who advised me to try giving them baby cereal, perhaps with a little honey. They liked it, but were too fastidious to eat it because it was sticky. (Groany nearly died of horror when anything sticky touched his immaculate whiskers.)

They seemed to have very delicate stomachs and were easily upset. One day Groany ate some chopped peanuts and immediately had a convulsion. In terror he reached out his little hands to me, and I took him and held him and thought he was dying, but in a little while he seemed all right again.

We were very cautious, therefore, in feeding them, giving them mashed or ground walnuts (a small amount), scraped apple and carrot, one seedless grape at a time. We never gave them bread or sugar, two things the naturalist had warned us about, though we caught all three stealing from the sugar bowl at times, especially Mimi, who had a *very* sweet tooth.

They were wild to get into the soil in my flower pots, so we brought a box of soil from the woods, and they spent hours digging and hunting in it, eating from it some sort of tidbits which we were never able to identify, but which they seemed to crave. The woods soil was fascinating, even to us, being full of tiny snail-shells, minute leaves, and bits of moss. After that, we brought them a fresh box of woods soil each month during the mild seasons.

When Mimi was about four months old, she began to look around for "a home of her own."

One day, as I opened a box of cleansing tissue, she snatched a piece of it and performed an amazing feat. Sitting up very straight, she took the tissue in both little hands and rolled it up under her chin, forming a little "pillow." This was not a slow or uncertain act, but was done in a flash, with the sureness born of instinct.

She then looked about for a place to put the pillow and decided upon a floor lamp in the den. Still holding it, but in her mouth, she ran up the lamp and arranged it neatly in the reflector bowl under the shade, putting it next to the light bulb. She then came down, seized another tissue, made another pillow, and went back up.

We disconnected the lamp, removed the light bulb and silk shade, and let Mimi have the reflector bowl for her own. She made a cosy nest in the bowl, first lining it with pillows, then shredding tissue to make it softer.

To do this, she sat up very straight, and placed her back feet firmly on the lower edge of a sheet of tissue. She then took the upper edge in her little hands and held the sheet taut. Now, working from bottom to top, she ripped the sheet into neat, even shreds with her teeth and carried them into the bowl in her mouth. With these, the pillows, and the small terry blankets we donated, she completed her new home and retired there to live in splendid isolation.

Though she came down to eat and play, she spent much of her time lying in the bowl, often dangling one arm over the side like a languid lady in her bath. Later Shad joined her there and they often took naps together, curled up with their arms around each other. One morning I heard them talking cosily and peeped in at them. They were lying in the bowl, facing each other. "*Crrrr-onk*," one would say. And the other would reply, "*Crrrrrrrrrr-onk*." It was interesting but most frustrating.

About this time I received a letter from a woman who lived in a small Indiana village, and whose name was Lamb. Mrs. Lamb had read about our little squirrels and had a fascinating story to tell about her own:

We were farmers for more than twenty years, and it fell to me to raise a number of bottle-babies, mostly pigs, calves, and kittens, but one summer day in the 1930s, my husband came to the house carrying three tiny squirrels in his hat. They were only a few days old, as their eyes were still closed, and there wasn't a hair on them.

I hardly knew how to begin to feed them. The only thing I had which was small enough to use was a medicine dropper. I can't remember that I made up any special formula for them, just warm milk with perhaps a little Karo added, but they were as tough as little pine knots and lived and grew.

We kept them in the kitchen in a big cardboard box with a screen over it, but it wasn't long until they were climbing up the sides and pushing out under the screen. After a few weeks I taught them to eat and drink from a saucer. We always hoped to get finished with our own meals before they began to scramble out but were not always successful, as they soon learned what the rattle of dishes meant.

They loved to be with us and were always following us. They would climb up on our laps, and leap upon the table so fast that we did well if we caught them before they were into a dish of something. They were hearty eaters and liked almost everything, but were especially fond of cottage cheese and butter. One morning, while cooking breakfast, I turned to the table and found one of them eating away on a pancake I had just made.

Unless you saw them with your own eyes, you would not believe the things they did. Many times I have watched them wash their faces, first wetting their hands as a cat does, and scrubbing chest and arms, too. Then they would reach around and get their bushy tails and use them as we would a towel.

We gathered a bushel of hickory nuts that fall, and set the basket near the range to dry. When the squirrels found them, they had the time of their lives with them. They would use their little hands to move a nut to the edge of the basket and over the side, then jump down to the floor and roll it away to a hiding place under a rug, under the kitchen cabinet, in an overshoe, wherever they could find a likely spot.

We had a squirrel-dog that was a good hunter, and we taught him not to harm these pets. Other squirrels, yes . . . but not *these* squirrels. He learned his lesson and would lie by the stove and watch them play on the kitchen floor, but would never bother them. The largest of our squirrels was a male, and he would growl deep in his throat when anything frightened him.

They were healthy and fat and we felt that we must find an outdoor home for them before winter came, a place where they could live a life of their own, store their food, and learn to provide for themselves. My husband found a good tree for them at the edge of the woods. He nailed a little "porch" on it and kept it filled with corn and nuts and other food for them.

I never saw them again, but they were always in my thoughts. Late the next spring, my husband was working near the woods when he saw a squirrel sitting on the ground, watching him. Our dog saw it too, and gave chase. The dog was very swift, but he had only chased this squirrel a short distance when he stopped and let it get away. He came back to my husband, wriggling all over, the way dogs do, as if trying to tell him something. We always believed it was one of our babies, that it came out to see my husband, and that the dog recognized it as one of the squirrels he had been taught not to touch.

Sophronia Lamb (Mrs. Ott Lamb)
Centerville, Indiana

Most people who wrote or talked to us about pet squirrels spoke of them with the sort of affection one usually reserves for a child. Once in a while, however, someone would say, "We had a squirrel once, kept him in a nice cage and fed him every day. But he got mean. . . ."

Whether this squirrel became "mean" because of cramped quarters, a faulty diet, or neglect, who can say? There is, of course, a great difference in people's ideas of what constitutes a "nice cage" *or* a good diet, but they are hardly to be blamed for their errors, considering that almost nothing is published to help them. Nor do they have any way of knowing that a pet squirrel may become "mean" for lack of play and love.

Squirrels need room to skip, hop, jump, turn, leap, romp, roll, run, and rebound. They need a place to bury little stores and dig them up again, to sit up and eat, to sleep in comfort, to stretch out prone and relaxed.

As for keeping them gentle and happy, it is the consensus of those who work with natural-history museums that such animals should be handled *every day* lest they cease to be tame. They need tenderness and affection, for they themselves are tender and affectionate toward their owners, and (except during eating and mating periods) toward each other. More than once we have seen Mimi tuck the other little ones in at night, pulling a "blanket" over them with her teeth, then patting it in place with her little hands.

Shad was probably one of the dearest and tenderest little animals that ever lived. He would come running to meet us, "laughing" the way a dog "laughs" and talking to us in many happy little *mm . . . mm . . . mm*'s. He was always the largest, gentlest, and most intelligent of the three, had a great love of play and a lively curiosity. When I found he was interested in playing with a certain Mexican bean pot, I put it down on the floor for him, and he used it as his special refuge. When he and Mimi played hide-and-seek, he would run and leap in the bean pot to hide, then rise up and peep out to see where she had gone. He took afternoon naps in Lee's size-eleven-and-a-half loafer, and often buried an English walnut there.

One morning I looked around just in time to see him busily eating some fall flowers out of a vase. I took the vase away from him (most of the flowers were gone), but didn't worry about him because Bill told me he had seen wild squirrels eat and relish chrysanthemums, roses, and violets, so I supposed they ate all sorts of flowers. Later, however, he was very quiet and I observed that he was sitting with his head lowered, something I came to learn was a symptom of illness.

Suddenly, he gave a sharp, sudden cry. Then he growled, deep in his throat, like a dog. I did not know then, but learned later, that this means terror. After that, he seemed all right for a while. Then he cried out again, leaped up, and ran wildly across the room. It is characteristic of these little animals to run when they feel pain, as if to escape or outdistance it, another thing I learned later on.

When I spoke to Shad, he came to me and I talked to him

and petted him. He grew quiet and seemed comforted. But he cried out again, and this time he was bent double. I realized that he was very ill, and suffering the symptoms of poisoning. The veterinarian, when I called, said to bring him to the office at once.

At regular and more frequent intervals, little Shad cried out as though in agony, but when the pain passed, he seemed all right, except that he looked weaker and sicker each time. When I called him, he came to me and crept into my lap and huddled in my arms as though he thought I could protect him from the horrible thing that had seized him and was torturing him.

All the way to the animal hospital he kept crying out at intervals in great pain. I was shaken by his agony, and by the fact that I did not know how to help him. (Worse, I did not know that a squirrel, in strange hands, may collapse and die of shock.)

I carried him into the examining room and laid him upon the table. He was suffering a great deal now, and kept reaching his little hands to me, clinging to me. Swiftly but gently, the doctor started to examine him, but the moment Shad felt and scented these great unfamiliar hands upon him, he gave a tremendous lurch and leaped to the floor. The effort was too much for him, and he was unable to get up again. He simply crawled, with his last strength, to where I stood, laid his little head upon my shoe, and died.

I don't think I ever cried more bitterly than when we buried Shad. I felt it was my fault that our tenderhearted little pet had died so tragically, that I should have learned more about caring for him, more about protecting him. But very little has been published about fox squirrels as mammals, and almost nothing about fox squirrels as pets. I had never dreamed that the flowers would hurt him because, at that time, I did not know so many garden flowers are poisonous.

I have heard a great many people say, and with great conviction, that *all* animals know instinctively which plants will harm and which will help them, which to eat and which to avoid. This, of course, is an error.

Years ago the cows of early Indiana settlers ate the deadly white snakeroot, and their milk consequently poisoned and killed large numbers of people. One of the victims was Nancy Hanks Lincoln, Abraham Lincoln's beloved mother, whose grave is in southern Indiana.

The settlers were frightened and baffled by this deadly malady, knowing only that it usually struck those who had drunk fresh milk. They called it "milk sickness" and its cause remained a mystery for years. White snakeroot still grows abundantly in the Indiana woods, and along streams or in moist valleys, and is responsible for the deaths of many farm animals every summer, as are other poisonous plants of the countryside. Such plants are not the first choice of grazing animals, but will be eaten when more palatable and harmless growth is scarce.

State-sponsored bulletins provide farmers with pictures and descriptions of dangerous growths, and give instructions for eradicating them. Sometimes city people who buy pasture lands for their saddle horses are not even aware of the existence of such plants, and lose valuable animals that have eaten harmless-looking leaves, bark, weeds, and flowers. Squirrels and other animals of the wilds avoid such plants, not because of instinct, but probably because their mothers taught them this lesson in survival, just as they taught them many more.

Perhaps if I had known more about garden flowers and less about wild flowers, Shad would not have died. Perhaps the fact that he was such a sensitive little creature caused him to go into shock more readily. We have since learned that any form of restraint may send a squirrel into a panic, may cause him to die of fright. Trapped squirrels often go into a daze, trappers say, convulse with fear, and expire in the "shock position" . . . head down, body bent. (This is believed to be the origin of the old back-country expression, "He just curled up and died," a phenomenon which settlers had witnessed many times, and which was very puzzling to them.)

Bill often told me how woods creatures, seized in the grip of an enemy, would simply go into shock and expire, and thus be saved further pain and terror. There is an old hunter's legend which says that the captive "wills itself to die" but he called this "storybook talk." No, he said, this form of death was nature's kindly way of putting the animal to sleep before it was torn apart by some beast of prey.

Mimi and Shad had played together all the time, and after he died, Mimi seemed lost and lonely. For some time she hunted him as she had done when they played hide-and-seek, looking under a cushion, into the cage, behind the door, down the Mexican bean pot. Then she hunted him no more. Until now, she had paid very little attention to Groany, except for gestures of motherly solicitude, and he looked and seemed so much younger than she that we often spoke of him as "the baby squirrel" though they were the same age.

Now that he could sit up and eat, could romp and run, and now that Mimi was lonely, he became her playmate. Each morning when she had awakened, had sat through her stupor, then washed and brushed herself (as little as possible), she descended from her bowl, ready for her breakfast. By this time Groany had been busy for hours, tending his immaculate whiskers, combing his sleek little head, brushing his tail, grooming his fur. As soon as he finished, he came up to me as though to be admired, and held up his head so that I could whisper to him.

"Never in all my born days have I seen a squirrel more elegant or more foppish than you!" I would whisper, all of which pleased him very much.

I always fixed their breakfasts on two little plates and fed both at the same time, so there would be no fuss. We knew from watching the wild squirrels at our feeder that they often quarreled over food, the larger ones chasing the smaller ones away and refusing them as much as a seed until their own appetites were appeased.

To a squirrel, the grass is always greener on the other side of the tree, and soon after we gave them their food, we would see them ignoring their own plates, each eyeing some tasty tidbit on the plate of the other. Mimi, who was a sly little wench and always full of tricks, soon learned that Groany could not see out of his left eye. She would therefore "tiptoe" around to his left side, then quick as lightning snatch a grape or a strawberry from his plate and run off with it.

With an outraged cry, Groany would lunge after her, and around and around the floor they went, a streak of fur and tails and rage, Mimi screaming with defiance (and, I think, with evil pleasure), Groany squalling with wrath. This chase-to-the-death continued, full of sound and fury, until Mimi dropped the treasured tidbit, Groany recaptured it, or they had mangled it enough for both to gobble some of it down.

Sometimes, when they were both in the cage, they would uncover a buried morsel such as a pecan, and fly into a furious quarrel over it, screaming, rolling, squawking, snatching it back and forth. I would march into the room and demand indignantly, "*What's going on in here?*" Instantly, two little heads went down on little hands, and both squirrels became as still as mice, thinking they were hidden from my displeasure, because they obviously believed that if they couldn't see *me*, I couldn't see *them*.

This theory they demonstrated constantly while playing around the house. Any new and unfamiliar object was regarded with vast suspicion and approached with the utmost caution. It might be only a book on the sofa, Lee's house slipper on the floor, a glove on the bed, even a paper wad by the desk. But anything new and different put them on their guard in an instant, just as it does in the woods, where they will notice a new stone in the path, a twig just broken, a shadow by the sycamore, which wasn't there this morning. (This is true, however, not only of animals, but of people accustomed to a familiar woods, who can instantly discern any alterations in the patterns of growth and trail around them, and can even detect the space left by a fallen hedge apple.)

Crouched down, belly close to the floor, Groany (like Mimi) would approach a suspicious object with small and cautious steps, prepared at every instant for flight. His tail, spread wide, shielded him from the "gaze" of the offender and, he seemed to think, hid him completely. Thus shielded, he would scoot past the enemy and view it with equal caution from another angle. After making a number of these wary approaches, and finding that the shoe neither moved nor attempted to charge him, he would saunter away as nonchalantly as though he had never feared it in the first place.

VI I once edited a national magazine for children, and during those years learned a great deal about pets. Children wrote to me from nearly every country in the world, and in my mail came thousands upon thousands of letters extolling the virtues of dogs, cats, mongooses . . . kiwi birds, myna birds, parakeets . . . woodchucks, fawns, small pigs, frogs, turtles, fish, skunks, raccoons, and others.

These pets were very often acquired by chance. Dad brought a baby rabbit from the wheat field after its mother had been killed by a mower . . . found a baby bear alone in the forest . . . discovered a lamb so frail it would die without special care . . . picked up a lost puppy that was cowering under the front porch, and so on.

Many kittens were rescued from stonings by tenderhearted little girls. Lost or abandoned dogs became the constant companions of children they had followed home. Birds that had tumbled from nests, and many other helpless little creatures, were given devoted care and love by small boys and girls.

Unkindness toward animals was shocking to most of my readers, and their feelings sometimes found expression in indignant verse. One little girl wrote:

Throwing rocks
At poor little helpless animals
Is only done by kids
That is savages and cannibals!

The most popular pet, I think, was the dog. Indeed, I have inspected thousands and thousands of photos which showed dogs submitting patiently, even joyfully, to the whims of their owners. There were dogs dressed in doll clothes . . . being wheeled in baby carriages . . . stuffed into a boy's hip pocket . . . riding in a bike basket . . . hanging from the clothesline in a stocking . . . peering out of the family mailbox . . . playing a piano . . . twirling a baton . . . wearing spectacles and holding a book . . . sitting on the back of a pony . . . sitting in a chair at a party table, sometimes even wearing a party hat. And far from appearing distressed or frightened, these dogs looked happy and proud.

Queer friendships grew up between dogs and cats, and between other animals. One child wrote about a pig and a dog who became inseparable companions. Another told of a friendship between her pet dog and her pet duck. When the duck was killed, the dog mourned at her grave for weeks.

Dog birthdays were gala events. The dogs were combed, bathed, brushed, and had ribbon bows tied to their collars. They had their own birthday parties and cakes, guests sometimes being other dogs, accompanied by *their* owners.

Names which the children gave to their pets were no indication of gender. "Pauline is my kitten. He is so sweet." . . . "Daisy is a wild squirrel, but he eats out of my hand. Perhaps you wonder how I can tell him from the other squirrels. It is because we are acquainted."

Many children had pet turtles, and insisted that the intelligence of these pets was truly remarkable. I was told that they leaped to meet their owners, could do wonderful tricks, and were often seen playing tag in the fishbowl (probably the slowest game on record). Turtles, the children insisted, had individuality and personality. They winked at shared jokes, blew bubbles by giggling. Some smiled broadly at their owners; others were said to have attempted speech. The owners declared their turtles knew their own names and would come when called. Most of them were named Myrtle the Turtle, and if a child owned more than one, rhyming names were attempted. One boy had "twins" called Myrtle and Hurtle. A little girl had "triplets," called the first two Myrtle and Hurtle and the third one Birtle, a name obviously chosen in desperation. Another little girl had a pair of turtles named Sloppy and Sleepy.

The love of children for their pets, the complete devotion between owner and animal, is of a depth incomprehensible to those who have never had the experience, and thus have missed one of the richest adventures in life. One little boy wrote, "My pet is a pedigreed airdale-scotty-terrier. He is a very fine dog." A little girl wrote proudly, "I have had my little dog ever since I got her." A boy said, "My dog is the best dog in our naborhood, and the strongest and the smartest and the fastest. And he would of won the race, if he had not et that dam cake." Perhaps the noblest tribute to a dog that I have ever read came in a letter from a little girl who owned a cocker puppy. It said: "I think she is just about all that is necessary."

Sometimes the dogs died, or were killed by speeding cars, and then the children poured out their grief in letters that, quite often, were literally smudged with tears. "My little dog that loved me so is dead, and my heart is broke."

This I understood when Cricket, our cocker, died and I went out into the country to bury her. Cricket was past ten, but it was hard to realize that, in the world of dogs, she was old, for she still had the excited joyousness, the supple motion, and the childlike eagerness of puppyhood.

When my husband was overseas and Jamie was away at school, the little black cocker was very comforting to me, and never left me for a moment. For some reason, she loved the sound of my typewriter and, as long as I was typing, would lie under my desk in quiet contentment.

When I was very busy, perhaps working against a deadline,

many days might pass before I saw anyone or talked to anyone except Cricket. Then my copy was finished and sealed and stamped, and I would take it down to be put on the night train. For a time I found companionship in the lights and bustle and voices at the station, then the train came and went, the track turned dark, and the world was suddenly still. The station, emptied, seemed to have closed its eyes. I would walk slowly back to the car, my steps echoing, strange and hollow, on the pavement, and then drive home along the empty streets and let myself into the empty house. For a moment I would stand there, tired and dispirited, looking at the clutter I must pick up and sort out and put back into the files. Then there would be a sound of little scuffling feet at the door, and Cricket would hurl herself into my arms. I would hold her close and lean my head against hers, and sitting there in the silence, we would share our loneliness.

Cricket was Jamie's dog and loved her dearly, but she loved Lee and me, too. Cricket was love, sweetness, fidelity, and charm, but no one could say she was brilliant. Her pedigree was as full of distinguished ancestors as the Hall of Fame, and so long that when I unrolled it, I felt like Benjamin Franklin getting ready to read the Declaration of Independence, but she never seemed smart enough to grasp the things a little dog is supposed to learn.

Once, when I was in the tub, she came trotting into the bathroom. I spoke one single stern word, the command we thought she had learned perfectly, "*Lie!*" She promptly jumped into the bubble bath with me, and the result resembled those African movies in which you see river water churning violently as an alligator devours a hapless native.

Jamie, however, considered her the most intelligent dog that ever lived and consoled her with words like, "Of *course* you're smart! Why, you're a *brilliant* little pet!"

With Jamie and Lee both gone, Cricket felt as lost and lonely as I felt, and we were seldom apart. I swept the porch, closely followed by Cricket, who trotted merrily through the sweepings. I listed the laundry, closely followed by Cricket, who lay down on top of it to rest. I sat down to my solitary dinner, while Cricket, who had hastily gulped her own food, sat up in front of me, waving her feathery paws and begging for mine. When I sat down to read, she cuddled against me. When I got into bed, she slept at my feet. If I was ill with a cold, she would trot to the bed a dozen times an hour, whimper softly, and lay her head down on my chest.

One night, after Jamie and Lee were home again, Cricket became very ill. Jamie sat up with her all night and Lee and I went in to her at intervals, but she did not respond to treatment, and in the morning she was much worse. At an early hour I wrapped her in a blanket and carried her to the animal hospital.

The veterinarian came and looked at her and told me she was dying. Two women, who seemed to be waiting to talk to him about advertising, looked at me curiously. I thought I sensed what they were thinking. *Too bad, but it is only a dog, and she can always get another dog.* They could never know all that Cricket and I had shared. I gathered her up and put my face against the top of her soft little head, for what I knew was the last time.

When she was gone, I placed her, still wrapped in her blanket, in a sturdy wooden box and tied it up with her leash. By that time Lee was at work. Jamie, worn out, was sound asleep and it seemed best to spare her the ordeal of Cricket's burial, which I had arranged with Marjorie.

I found Marjorie waiting for me at the edge of the woods with her two sons, Bob and Denny. Being boys, they loved and understood dogs and they knew what it was like to lose one, for only a little while before, their own dog had been struck by a speeding car and left to die on the roadway as she tried to drag herself home. They had dug Cricket's grave near hers and, being tenderhearted, had picked some May flowers to lay upon it and brought a flat stone from the creek to mark it.

The boys helped me to bury her. Afterward, I stood in the bright spring stillness of the woods and looked back at the quiet little mound under the redbud tree and knew that, of all the lonely moments Cricket and I had shared, this was the loneliest.

We never had another dog, but pets somehow find their way into the lives of people who love them, and we were not exceptions. Some of the pets who found their way to us, however, were uninvited and wholly unanticipated. There was a large number of "transient pets" picked up injured or lost, wild creatures which after being fed, comforted, and healed were released in Marjorie's woods. There was a small owl struck by a car, an indigo bunting that suffered a similar fate, an injured bunny, a young possum found cowering and bewildered on Main Street. We could only surmise that he had fallen asleep on the under-carriage of a farm truck (a possum habit) and awakened only after the truck came to town.

Given a respected place in our pet lore was The Mystery of the Rhode Island Reds, an enigma unsolved to this day.

One very early summer morning, the cleaning woman who was helping me came in and said in a shaken voice, "Miz Kellner, there's a chicken peeping in at the front window." I went in and looked and found a small Rhode Island Red pullet curled up on a living-room window sill.

The moment I went out and spoke to her, she flew down from this perch and came to me, looking up at me and talking eagerly in the crooning language of a pet hen, "*Crrrrrrrrr . . . crrrrrrrr . . . crrrrrrrr.*" When I went inside, she wanted to go in with me, so I felt sure that she *was* a pet and had belonged to a woman, or perhaps a girl.

We cared for her until we were certain that nobody was going to claim her. Then we took her to my uncle's farm in the country, where she became a favorite of the family.

Almost a year to the day after this happened, Jamie came in and said to me, "I hate to mention it, but history repeats itself. There's a chicken peeping in at the front window."

I went back into the living room and there on the same window sill sat another Rhode Island Red pullet, the same size and color of the one that had appeared just as mysteriously the previous year. I went out and spoke to her, and she came to me with the same "*Crrrrrr . . . crrrrrrrrr . . . crrrrrrrr*" talk, and wanted to follow me inside. It gave me an eerie sensation of having gone back in time.

We fed, welcomed, and cared for her as for the other one, until we were certain that nobody was going to claim her. Then we took her out to my uncle's farm, where we had some difficulty convincing him that, with absolutely no encouragement from us, the same thing had happened twice. However, he accepted the newcomer hospitably enough, and she also became a family favorite.

As for the unsolved mystery, there have been several theories about it, the least plausible that these pullets escaped from poultry trucks which halted at the stoplight on their way to a Cincinnati market, and just wandered to the house nearest the corner.

Our own theory is that both these pullets were Easter gifts to some child, possibly a little girl. The first time the gift-chick grew old enough to venture into the world by itself, it had wandered away and become lost, and somebody said, "Never mind. I'll get you another one next year," and did. Counting from an Easter hatching, both would have reached pullet age by the time they came to us. But how they happened to wander away at the same time of the month, choose the same house, same window, and same family is inexplicable. Children who lived in India used to write to me about their patron saint of animals. I forget his name now, but he was supposed to guide lost, injured, and hungry creatures to people who would care for them. All I can say is: he's been busy as a bee around here.

The little owl we rescued was delivered to Marjorie, who did her best to feed it before she returned it to the woods. Patiently, she offered it choice portions of hamburger, but it ate nothing. At last she telephoned a naturalist, who explained that because of the structure of its beak, an owl is able to eat only food that it can tear. So Carl, being of the stronger sex, brought it a dead mouse out of a trap and it instantly pounced upon this tasty dinner and others like it.

Some weeks later I met the grizzled mountaineer on the street, and when he stopped and asked how the squirrels were faring, I told him about the owl, too.

"Say now!" he commented, his face brightening. "That puts me in mand of what heppened to me and my waff. Eight-nan months back, I heerd a quarr noise at the winder one nat, and me and my waff, we lewked out, and guiss whote was thar? A laytle scritch-ale!"

The little screech owl, he continued, was matty kewt, but wouldn't eat a thing. Just set there, die after die, got more droopified, and pore as a snek. Finally, he got up the narve to go see a perfesser, and learned what Marjorie had learned, that an owl must tear its food. So he took the laytle critter to the perfesser, and the perfesser fed it till it fleshed-up, and then let it go. Most mountain people have, I have found, like many other hunters, a great interest in wildlife, a keen knowledge of it, usually, and a great tenderness toward little wild creatures that are lost and helpless.

Among our foundlings were two small pets alien to Indiana soil, a pair of horned toads picked up on the Mexican border. It was hot there when we left, about the middle of April, but very cold in Indiana, and snowing when we arrived home. The toads, which we had brought along, were flattened out in their box with their eyes closed, icy to the touch, and absolutely stiff. I thought in horror, Ye gods, the poor little things have frozen to death! But later I learned that this is their normal reaction to cold. Once they were warm again, they became as lively as though they were still under a Texas sun.

A horned toad is really a type of lizard, said to be "horned" because of the protective spikes around its head, which *may* keep snakes from seizing and eating him. I would never say that I consider horned toads the most fascinating of pets, but they *are* interesting, and ours, loaned to elementary teachers, were sources of awe and wonder to school children who had never seen the like.

Horned toads eat insects, especially ants, are lively in summer, will hibernate in winter. One summer day Lee took them out into the back yard, and put them near an ant hill to feed. Just then a paper boy stopped to make his weekly collection and happened to glance down at them. He dropped everything, including his money.

"*Mister!*" he gasped. "Look down cher feet! Don't let 'em git away! I'll run and git a jar!"

Many people have owned a pet cricket, and most people are fascinated by this lively little creature of the night. All sorts of folkways and superstitions have grown up around him, and his nocturnal song (made by rubbing his forewings together) suggests cheer and companionship to some listeners, loneliness and sadness to others.

We used to say, in back-country Indiana, that if you killed a cricket, there would be no rain. We also said that a cricket singing in the house brought good luck. If you fear it will nibble the linens, carry it out of the house and gently slip it into some weeds, but do not kill it unless you want misfortune to befall you, and soon.

We learned that, before a storm, the singing of crickets grew louder and faster, though we did not know the reason. Actually all sounds are clearer before "falling" weather because on cloudy and humid days and nights, the acoustical wave (sound) is bent back to earth instead of being dissipated, and can be heard farther, as well as more distinctly. And crickets always chirp faster when the weather is hot. To accurately determine the temperature, count a cricket's chirps for fifteen seconds, then add forty to that number.

In the Orient, crickets are commonly kept as pets, put into cages of their own, sometimes fed from their own tiny dishes. But we never thought of crickets as pets until, out of curiosity as well as interest, we went to visit a "cricket ranch" in Memphis.

This "ranch," where gray crickets are raised for bait, was a large building, rather macabre in appearance since it seemed to be full of coffins. These, however, were the carefully controlled incubators in which the crickets were hatched and brought up, and contained different ages, different sizes, all chirping loudly. The little creatures are raised with much care and attention to temperature and humidity, feeding, shelter, prevention and treatment of illness.

I was given a handful of crickets as a present, all males, since the females do not "sing." It is easy to distinguish between the sexes, as females have a long needle-like "tail" (ovipositor) through which their eggs are pushed into the ground.

Crickets must have coolness, shelter, and dampness, as they quickly die in too much heat or sun. We put ours in a large deep bowl, where they sang happily through the dark winter days. To give them water, I filled a shallow lid and set it in the middle of the bowl. The crickets immediately gathered around it, like little horses around a trough, drinking, drinking, and drinking. As the cricket ranch suggested, we gave them starting mash, the kind used for baby chicks, and they seemed to relish it. Eventually they quietly died, as their life span ended, one or two at a time.

On snowy evenings, it was not uncommon for a friend to drop in, sit a while, look embarrassed, and finally say, "It's strange . . . but for a moment . . . well, it sounds awfully silly, I know . . . but I could have *sworn* I heard crickets. . . ."

One of nature's most interesting pets came our way very unexpectedly on a pleasant summer evening.

A little boy named Jimmy, who lived down the street, asked me to go with him while he walked his dog in the park. We were strolling along the path in the soft darkness, when suddenly he stopped beneath a light and, from the beech tree beside him, picked a leaf with an object on it.

"What's *this?*" he asked, with something like revulsion.

I looked and saw that it was a large smooth caterpillar, looking a little like a dragon, but very beautiful with its pale-green skin, tufted and decorated with brilliant Chinese-red designs.

"I'm not sure," I said, "but I *think* this may be the caterpillar of a very beautiful moth called the P-o-l-y-p-h-e-m-u-s moth."

I then explained that this word was pronounced Pol-i-*fee*-mus, and was the name of a one-eyed giant in Greek legends, and that the moth had been named for him because it seemed to have one eye on each wing.

"He's very interesting," I said, holding him out, into the light.

"I know God made him," gulped Jimmy, who was a very religious little boy. "But why did God make him so *sickening?*"

I told Jimmy that if he would watch the caterpillar eat and prepare for winter, I felt sure he would find it less repulsive, and next spring he would see it changed into a lovely moth. So we took it home, with some leaves from the beech tree, breaking off a few low branches. Lee put these branches in an old milk bottle half full of water, and set the caterpillar in the midst of them. He reared up and jerked his head back into one of his segments (which gave him a weird hooded appearance) and clicked his jaws menacingly, as at his enemies.

Soon afterward, though, he settled down and began to eat,

and from then on, we were rushing like mad to keep up with his appetite. He ate night and day, biting off leaves with the cutters in his mouth, chewing them up with the grinders. He sounded as if he were chewing, chewing, chewing, without an instant's pause. I would wake in the night and hear him chewing, and in the morning, the twigs would be bare.

We offered him several kinds of leaves, but only beech leaves pleased him, and the nearest beech was four blocks away. We rushed down and broke off more branches, rushed back and fed the caterpillar. All day he chewed. At night, we went to get more leaves. All night he chewed. Came morning, more bare branches, and a rush for more leaves. He ate and ate and *ate*, until we thought his skin would burst, which indeed it does, from time to time. When a caterpillar grows too big for his skin, he simply waits for a new one to grow, discards and eats the old one, and starts on more leaves.

Before long, the days began to grow chilly, and one morning when there was frost on the ground, I no longer heard the caterpillar chewing. Down one side, he had joined the edges of two beech leaves together with a silken substance from his mouth, making a little canoe-shaped cradle, himself inside. He then sealed the open side of the leaves together, so that he was encased for the winter.

Gently we lifted the twig on which his cocoon hung and slipped it into a vase in a warm room. And there it remained while the weather grew colder and snow came, and winter blasts blew, and icicles hung at the windows.

All the books said these moths came out in the spring, so I did not expect to see ours before then. He emerged, however, strong and full grown at Thanksgiving time, due to the warmth of the house.

At the time I had gone to take a pumpkin pie to two frail old ladies. (It is a bitter thing to me that every time I go on an errand of mercy, something happens to make me wish I had stayed at home!) Lee noticed that the cocoon had begun to jerk and bounce in a very agitated manner, and presently a hideous little thing came out of it, looking like a wet worm with ragged, malformed wings. He had never witnessed the metamorphosis of a moth, and thought in horror, "Good Lord, he's come out too soon!"

The wretched little object made its way to the strongest twig in the vase and hung there, a position which pulls its wings down and allows them to harden properly as the body fluid is pumped into them. (If they failed to harden properly, he would be unable to fly.) As the transformation continued, lasting for about half an hour, Lee stood glued to the spot, unable to turn away from the miracle before his eyes, hardly able to believe it.

He watched the wings lengthen and unfold, the body shorten, the antennae grow into twin ferns. The velvety fur which covered the moth grew dry, the beautiful colors became clear, and the great yellow and purple "eyes" could be seen. In an hour or so, the moth began to move his wings, and everything was over just as I got home again. Had this been a summer evening, he would have flown out into the darkness, mated, and died, but since it was winter, he spent his brief life with us.

A number of people, especially children, consider insects fascinating pets. When Marjorie's son Bob was about twelve years old, he came upon an exceptionally large and colorful fly and decided to make a pet of it, a decision which his mother reversed as soon as she heard about it. She found that he had attached a long string to the fly with a bit of airplane glue and was strolling behind it singing "Where He Leads Me I Will Follow," which he had learned in Sunday school the week before.

Many people become greatly attached to pet parakeets and love them dearly, but I was never much impressed by them. When I visited a friend who had a pet parakeet, she would inform me proudly, "Budgie can talk as well as we can!" Budgie would then say, "Burble, burble, cheep, cheep," and my friend would cry, "Isn't that wonderful? He said: *'I'm so happy to meet you, do come back for lunch on Thursday!'* " But as far as I was concerned, Budgie had said, "Burble, burble, cheep, cheep," and made a botch of *that!*

Then I met a young man who owned a very smart little parakeet that he had spent many hours in training, working with it late at night, when everything was quiet and they were alone. It spoke clearly and strongly, and said things like, "Have a care, my proud beauty!" or, "What, ho, my good fellow!" When a surprised visitor turned to look at it, it would add demurely, "This is silly. Birds can't talk."

Consternation entered the household of a certain Quaker leader in our town when the son of the family acquired a parakeet named Chester. This little pet had been taught to say, "Chester is a bad bird," but he spoke his one line so poorly that it came out, "Chester is a bastard." Hence, Chester was always being rushed unceremoniously from the room when a dignified caller arrived.

I once had a pair of Zebra finches which were very cute, and which I carried home all the way from Key West. They were black and white (as their name would indicate), with bright orange beaks and feet, and the little male had an orange-red circle on either side of his little face. They lived in a small finch-cage, and slept in a gourd which hung from the "rafters." Their names were Frankie and Johnny.

Johnny went to bed at an early hour, hopping into the gourd through a hole cut in one side, and settling down on the piece of folded tissue I put there every day. But Frankie liked to stay up late and would continue to swing dreamily. Every now and then her mate, who had a rather surly disposition, would stick his head out of the gourd and chirp shrilly, commanding her to join him.

Sometimes she obeyed at once, but on other evenings he would have to call several times, more angrily each time.

When at last they were both in the gourd, I would invade their privacy by peeping in at them. Nothing could be cuter, I thought, than these two tiny birds close together and sound asleep.

Like so many creatures of the wilds, Johnny refused to share his food with his mate. When she came forward, timidly enough, and tried to take as much as one seed, he would fly at her in rage, squawk loudly, and flop her brutally with his wings, allowing her only the leftovers.

Once he had finished his meal, he became sleepy and hopped into the swing for a nap. Later she would join him there and sit meekly beside him while he swayed and rocked until his eyes closed. As soon as he was really asleep, she would turn on him suddenly and push him out of the swing. He would land on the floor of the cage awake, astonished, and squawking, but when he scrambled up, she was swaying as meekly as before, and he probably never knew what had happened.

We now have Pete, a canary with bright yellow feathers, a little gray cap, and a voice of liquid loveliness. Pete is a very alert and intelligent little fellow, and is quick to inform us (with a certain sharp call) if he is in need of more food or water. At night he lulls himself to sleep with a soft, drowsy, murmurous singing like that of the birds in the wilds at sunset. Hearing this, I am filled with nostalgia, thinking of Bill and those long-ago evenings when we sat on some wooded hillside and watched the colors fade in the sky and listened to what he called "the sleepy songs" of nesting birds.

Sometimes Pete will suddenly utter a shrill alarm cry and keep repeating it with the persistence and precision of a radar signal. Then I know that a cat has invaded our premises, and rush outside to evict it. How he discovers the presence of this intruder is a mystery. The cat is often beyond his range of vision, and since he has no such sense of smell, he could not have detected it by its odor. Possibly his extremely acute hearing has enabled him to identify its movements in the grass.

Various pets came and went in our household, but after we found the squirrels we gave most of our attention to them, and loved them more than any others except Cricket. We spent many hours playing with them, and I spent many hours watching them, making notes about them, trying to learn more about their needs and the proper way to care for them. I wrote to naturalists, zoos, colleges, museums of natural history, and other sources asking for advice, and nearly every answer I received echoed that already familiar phrase, "Not much is known. . . ."

I looked in many places for information about them, found little that was helpful, and much that was incorrect.

Many references did not discuss the fox squirrel at all, and when they did they said something like: "The fox squirrel is clumsy and not very fast. He does not hibernate in winter, but remains quietly inside his home. The mating season is in spring and the females produce two babies per litter. The call is a loud bark. Food consists of seeds, acorns, and young birds. Some live in leaf-nests all year round and some in knotholes. They are extremely destructive . . ."—all of which is either misleading or inaccurate. Such material, supposed to be authoritative, reminded me of Claude's dry comment, "Books know damn little about squirrels."

Watching Mimi and Groany, we saw them take on the protective coloring of fall. Their backs retained the dark bark-color of summer branches, but their underneath parts, including the underside of their tails, became the tawny color of autumn leaves. Little Mimi was as bright as a maple leaf. As winter approached, their coats grew grayer and their backs were powdered with white, like snow on bark.

They loved and trusted us now, but they were still creatures of the wild, and sometimes the wild quality in their natures dominated all else. Mimi, suddenly frightened by some unfamiliar sound, would panic and run, streak under the sofa or up a drapery, and freeze there. At such times, she would respond to no word from us, however gentle and reassuring, but remained staring and remote, as though she neither saw us nor heard us, did not even know us. She relaxed and came back to us only after the frightening sound had ceased, and she had had plenty of time to recuperate from her fears. As she grew older and more domesticated, however, these periods of flight and terror came less often, and finally they ceased altogether. Groany, who firmly believed I was his mother, would run to me if anything alarmed him, hide his head in my hand or under my sleeve.

Though they were always climbing into our laps, sitting on our shoulders, and nuzzling our cheeks in great affection, we soon learned that we could not pick them up and hug them as if they were kittens. Restraint terrified them, and they would instantly struggle to escape, or make desperate leaps for freedom. They wanted to be held very loosely, and under these circumstances, would purr happily.

There were times, too, when they wanted to be left alone and would warn us to keep away from them. This was done by a certain look in the eye, difficult to explain, impossible to describe. I really can't say how we knew it—but *we knew,* and so would anyone else. This warning usually came when they were trying to hide a nut, perhaps out of an instinctive fear of being robbed. After a while, however, such apprehension was wholly forgotten, and we were warned no more.

In the fall their appetites seemed heavier and their storing instincts accelerated. I watched Mimi and Groany scampering about with nuts, burying them in all corners, and watched the wild squirrels burying nuts outside. Out-of-doors, a squirrel may spend a whole day burying a nut, digging it up, carrying it to a new spot, burying it again.

He first digs a shallow hole with his front claws, puts the nut in it, scoops soil and leaves over it, and pats them down smoothly with his little hands, one of the cutest of his habits. In a little while, though, he comes running back, sure that he can find a better hiding place, scratches the nut out of the ground, picks it up in his mouth, and starts over somewhere else. He appears to be very busy and provident, but actually he is just wasting time. I have watched the same squirrel bury the same nut over and over, all afternoon.

We never gave the outside squirrels whole nuts because if we did, they would bury them instead of eating them, even when they were hungry. So we cracked all nuts before putting them out for our squirrels, and if they left any at all, the birds were delighted, for a great many birds like nut meats.

Many times we have heard people ask, "How *do* squirrels remember where they bury their stores?" The answer is that of course they don't. It is not necessary. The squirrel is equipped with a superior sense of smell, and uses it to locate stores buried during the winter months, his own or those of some other squirrel, it makes no difference. The stores of nuts buried in the ground appear to be communal, and whoever finds them is welcome to them. (Some are never found at all, and grow into trees.) In winter we have many times watched a squirrel make his way across the frozen ground, stop, sniff, then suddenly and unerringly dig through snow, leaves, dirt, and stones to extract a nut hidden months before that day.

Perhaps females are, by nature, more cautious and more provident than the males. Whenever we fed our pets, Groany would begin eating at once, but Mimi, no matter how hungry she might be, would always bury the first bite of everything in her bowl. Later, while she was busy playing, I would remove these tidbits from her nice clean blankets, leaving perhaps a few sunflower seeds or a couple of nut meats for a snack.

Squirrels love corn, especially green corn, but we did not give it to ours that first fall, thinking they might be too young to tolerate it. They had small pieces of butternut squash, which they loved, a bit of peach, tomato, apple, or some grapes. They were especially fond of watermelon, and Mimi would clutch her piece so tightly that the juice ran off her elbows and we had to wash her clean with a washcloth. Groany preferred the seeds, would slip away and hide them as if they were very valuable, then eat them "in secret."

It is a common mistake to believe that the diet of squirrels is made up wholly of nuts. Actually, the greater part of their diet consists of fruits and vegetables, seeds and succulent plants. Bill told me he had seen them eating wild garlic, and whenever I used garlic in a dish for dinner, I noticed that they seemed attracted to it. Sometimes I gave each of them a tiny sliver which they seemed to relish, though Groany was far too fastidious to enjoy anything even slightly sticky.

Some observers say that squirrels will gnaw bones, and Marjorie reported that she had witnessed this, especially with ham bones. We believed they were seeking salt and calcium, for we had once found Mimi sitting up with a salt shaker in her little hands, blissfully licking the top. After that we gave them a little salt now and then, allowing them to lick it from the palms of our hands with their tiny tongues. Groany showed a desire to nibble plaster, and both he and Mimi had pounced upon eggshells as though discovering rare delicacies. So we bought some calcium tablets for them and they ate one occasionally, as happily as children eating ice cream.

People asked us, "Aren't they destructive?" Certainly they would gnaw anything they came upon if allowed to do so. But when we gave them fresh sticks to chew (cut from the mulberry tree), they were less inclined to bother other things. We called these sticks "lollipops" and our pets found them as pleasing as candy.

VII Perhaps they could smell the squirrels in our house and therefore were reassured. It is hard to say. But the wild squirrels came to our feeder in great numbers, and appeared to be much more tame, after Groany and Mimi joined us.

If the feeder was empty when a squirrel arrived, he would promptly and unerringly come to the room where we happened to be at that moment. One morning, before we were out of bed, we were awakened by a scratching at the bedroom window screen, and there was a little squirrel going up and down, peering in. A squirrel came to the breakfast-room window, where Lee and I were having coffee, and we knew that the feeder was empty *again*. We can only surmise that they located us by scent.

A young and very timid squirrel sometimes played alone in the tree outside Jamie's window, and she often left nuts on the sill for him. One day she came down, very startled, to tell us that she had forgotten to put the food out, and when the little squirrel came, he *knocked* on the pane to remind her. How this knocking was accomplished, she could not say, but she thought it was done by pushing one hand against the glass—a possibility, since a squirrel's hands are very bony.

Squirrels, as Bill so often insisted, are a great deal smarter than people have believed, and some are surprisingly good at figuring things out. Groany and Mimi soon learned that a knocking sound at the door would bring us, and they would summon us by knocks accomplished in various ways. I have seen Mimi push against the French doors with her hand, causing them to rattle with a "knocking" sound. Groany rattled them by seizing the bottom of the door in his teeth, holding on to the lengthwise strip that covered the closure. Once, when he wanted me to open the bedroom door, I heard a very sharp knocking outside, and found he had a whole English walnut in his mouth and was banging the shell against the floor. Silently I apologized to Mr. Dubbs, for thinking him dotty when he said squirrels knocked on doors and windows for admission and attention.

One day, when I went to a luncheon, the guests asked me a number of questions about our wild pets. One woman said suddenly, "My mother once had a pet squirrel, a little thing she found out in the yard, crying. She rescued it, brought it up, and named it Susie, and was simply silly about it. When Susie grew up, my mother put her in a little house in the maple tree by our front door, and after a while she found a mate and had babies. Then one day Susie came to the door and knocked . . . you know how they do! . . . and when my mother opened the door, there she sat, so proud, with her three little ones in front of her. She had brought them especially to show Mother, and after Mother admired them, she carried them back to the nest."

This was so interesting to me, and sounded so natural, that I was wholly unprepared for the sly looks and furtive smiles exchanged by some of the other women. Knocked on the front door—a squirrel? *Now, really!*

And I had to admit that Mr. Dubbs was right about something else. "*You* can't divide up squirrels like they was apples!" *They* would choose their owners, he had said, and Mimi certainly did. She was supposed to be Jamie's pet, and Jamie had tended her devotedly, but like her mother before her, Mimi loved Lee most. Before she was six months old, all her affection and loyalty had been transferred to him, and when he came in from work, a little after five, she would stand up in her bowl and hold her arms up to him like a child begging to be taken.

We now gave Groany a sleeping bowl of his own. We tried a deep plastic bowl first, but when we found him nibbling the rim, we exchanged it for a large metal mixing bowl which was anchored to the floor of the cage, and lined with the little terry blankets.

Sometimes he slept in it and sometimes he didn't, as he really preferred a certain channel-back chair in the living room. This chair had a Granny afghan over the arm, and he cuddled beneath that and spent many nights in this cosy spot. Sometimes, in the afternoon, he took a nap under a sofa cushion. His eccentricities made it necessary for us to receive guests with something like, "Oh, please don't sit in *that* chair! There might be a squirrel in it!"

We let them sleep in bowls in order to watch their incredible sleeping postures, which few people have ever seen. Even people who own pet squirrels usually let them go into a box or log for sleeping, completely out of sight. We peeped in at Groany and Mimi many times each evening, sometimes even lifting their top blankets to look at them. After they became accustomed to these invasions of privacy, they did not even open one eye, though squirrels, by nature, are light sleepers.

Groany often slept on his back with his fingers interlaced upon his fat little tummy. Now and then he slept with a thumb in his mouth, even sucking it. Mimi usually slept on her back with her arms crossed neatly, a hand on each shoulder. Sometimes, however, she slept on her side with her cheek upon her bent arm, or against one hand, in the sweet posture of a little girl. Once in a while they had nightmares, kicking and crying out, as puppies do. There were times when they didn't want to go to bed and fought sleep like stubborn children, trying to hold their eyes open to see more of the fascinating motion of television. When they did sleep, they slept *instantly*, which was always very startling, as they appeared to have dropped dead.

Both learned their names and would usually come obediently when called. Mimi was always the first to answer, however, and wherever she might be when she heard her name, she would come out at once and look up at me as if saying, "Well, here I am! What do you want?"

If Groany was too "busy" to come, he would answer by scratching lightly on floor or wall or shelf, as the case might be. One day, after I had called his name, I listened carefully and heard a tiny scratching sound from the closet in our bedroom. He was not allowed in the closet, but I suppose I had left the door open, and the temptation to explore was too much for him.

I looked in and there he sat in an old hat which Lee had left upside down on the upper shelf. It was such a hat as every husband owns, battered and shapeless, which his wife hates but cannot persuade him to throw away. Now I saw that Groany was taking neat little bites out of the brim, leaving a unique scalloped effect. Much pleased, I closed the door and left him to his labors.

The hearing of fox squirrels is very acute, and it is not surprising that they soon learn their names. A certain Mr. Battles told me that he and his wife once owned a pair of squirrels named Mickey and Dickey. As easily as these names could be confused, Mickey never answered when they called Dickey, and Dickey never came when they called Mickey.

Mickey, Mr. Battles said, chose to belong to him, and Dickey chose Mrs. Battles. He believed (as do some other squirrel fanciers I have met) that it is characteristic for a male to choose a woman or girl owner, and for a female to prefer a man or boy.

Once when he tried to carry Mickey into the next room,

she fought and kicked and screamed at him, and at last he gave her a sharp spank which offended her very much. She sprang down as they entered the room, ran to where Dickey sat, and huddled against him.

"And told him about the spank!" declared Mr. Battles, firmly. "Oh, they've got a way of telling things to each other, all right! I don't know how they do it, but they do. And I *know* she told Dickey, because *he* turned his back on me too, and neither one of them spoke to me the rest of the day." He added confidantly, "You know how they turn their backs."

We did, indeed. If we stayed away all day and left them locked in their cage, they were highly insulted and would have none of us when we returned. No matter how we coaxed or wheedled, they turned their backs to us and remained coldly aloof, sulking as dogs sometimes sulk.

As for "telling things," we often saw them moving their mouths in what looked like some form of communication inaudible to us, though it may have been nothing more than animal grimaces. When they were angry with us, however (usually after being deprived of something they wanted to chew), they made violent and comical mouth movements which resembled silent swearing.

Groany and Mimi took very good care of their tails, grooming them several times a day. A squirrel's tail serves many important purposes. It is a towel, a blanket, a shield, a defense mechanism. It helps him to maintain his balance in the trees, and keeps him from being hurt when he falls. It screens him from his enemies and, when he puffs it up, may frighten them away. It protects him from the wind on chilly days and covers him warmly in his nest on winter nights. By throwing it across his eyes when he sleeps on a branch, he can shut out the disturbing light of the sun.

A squirrel uses his tail as a means of communication in a language all its own. If he flips it lightly, toward another squirrel, or toward his owner, he means, "Come on, let's play a game!" He may jerk it briefly when something or somebody disturbs his sleep, as if to say, "Oh, go away and be quiet!" He jerks it furiously and gives quick sharp barks, scolding an intruder, or taking offense at some suspicious object. But when he is really enraged, his tail goes round and round, a violent motion accompanied by loud chattering.

Some naturalists believe that a squirrel who loses his tail will not live long, so important is it to his welfare. However, many wild squirrels lose at least the tip of their tails in woods accidents or in combat. I have seen a number of squirrels with three quarters of a tail, half a tail, even less, the result of a narrow escape from a dog, a beast of prey, or a human being.

Nature has given the squirrel, for his own protection, a tail that can lose quite a bit of its length without causing him much bleeding or pain. When he is caught by the tail and springs free, fur and skin are sheared off the bone, leaving a stub which he then bites off, apparently without pain. If he loses much of the length, however, he must be considered a cripple, for he will be hampered in many ways all the rest of his life. Instinctively, perhaps, he must sense the importance of his tail, for he gives it fastidious and unfailing care, even when he is a lick-and-promise type like Mimi.

We soon discovered that our pets were charmed by musical sounds such as a clock, a chime, a church bell. They would stand on their hind feet, stretch up tall, and listen in child-like wonder. They were delighted with music, and whenever I had a lot of work to do and wanted to keep them from bothering me, I would perch them on a chair and put a record on the record player—something with a good beat, like a tango. Side by side, as quiet as good little children, they would listen for hours, just as they would watch the motion of television.

It is not surprising that squirrels are so often found in old attics and warehouses, for they simply *love* a clutter of any kind. When I was cleaning and had a great many things piled in a heap, perhaps on the stairway, Groany was enchanted. He would immediately establish himself in the midst of this mess and sit there as though on a throne.

He loved the linen cupboard in the back hall and was always trying to get into it. The doors, which reached almost to the floor, did not lock, and he soon learned to pull them open by seizing the lower edges in his teeth. He would then climb up into the shelves and sit in grand style among the towels and washclothes. When I came to look for him, he would hide under the nearest towel and keep as quiet as a mouse, for he really understood that the linen cupboard was forbidden territory. But his long bushy tail betrayed him to me, as the long bushy tails of wild squirrels so often betray them to hunters. He protested with loud screeches when I removed him, but never attempted to bite me, because I was his mother.

Another device which we used to keep them busy and quiet was the drawer of an old kitchen table. This we filled with all sorts of harmless odds-and-ends—bottle tops, little spoons, small empty boxes, wooden blocks, orange sticks, even paper wads. Squirrels have an absolutely insatiable curiosity, love to explore and examine things. When Lee brought home a package, Groany had to find out what was in it. If I beat a bowl of cake batter, Mimi had to climb up and see what I was doing. They followed us around all day, watching, inquiring, snooping, poking, investigating, and the kitchen drawer was a delight to them. They could rummage all they liked, snatch up favored objects and scamper off to hide these in their bowls. Later, we retrieved such treasures and put them back in the cluttered drawer, to be used all over again.

When our pets were new to us, we were puzzled by the fact that their baths were always accompanied by sniffing and sneezing sounds. Later, we discovered that this was because the moisture came, not from their mouths, but from their noses. A squirrel's mouth is dry, which enables him to spit out seeds and skins, and he is unexcelled as a spitter and peeler. Mimi could peel a grape in nothing flat, flip the seeds and skins out with her tongue. A squirrel's tongue is soft and almost dry and feels like a tiny warm feather, as I had every reason to know, for Groany was always licking my hand like a puppy. Being compulsive peelers, just as raccoons are compulsive launderers, squirrels are quick to discover and discard anything extraneous. If they found Band-aids on our fingers, and calluses on our thumbs, they set to work with great determination and devotion to remove them.

A squirrel's front teeth are long and sharp incisors, two above and two below. These are the instruments he uses for peeling fruits and vegetables, and for grinding nutshells to dust. The grinding helps to keep his incisors short, which is fortunate, for they grow very rapidly. Mimi was so devoted to Lee that she let him open her mouth and look down her throat whenever he liked, and this gave us a fine view of an interior seldom revealed to human eyes.

Mimi usually went to bed soon after sunset, tucking herself into her lamp bowl and sleeping under numerous blankets. Groany, however, liked to stay up late and would follow at my heels until I went into the living room and sat down to watch the television. Then he climbed upon my lap and watched, too, sometimes staying up as late as nine o'clock—late indeed for him.

When he grew sleepy, he would put himself to bed. It was a long, *long* walk to his cage, for a small squirrel, and often he was so sleepy that he staggered as he went; his eyes kept falling shut, and his little knees buckled under him. Reaching the cage at last, he would climb groggily into it, pull the covers over himself, and sleep *at once.*

Though Lee and Jamie said he was as spoiled as an overprotected child, I often took pity on him and let him ride to his cage on my shoulder. Later, he learned to wait until one of us got up to go to the kitchen, and would "hitch a ride" to his destination. Finally both he and Mimi learned to tell us when they wanted a ride, by making bouncy little movements as if preparing to jump.

Both were awake early in the morning and late in the afternoon, but slept through the middle of the day. Some natural-history accounts say that squirrels sleep upside down, but ours never did, though Groany often curled up in such a way that his head was lower than the rest of his body. At other times he arranged his blankets so that one of them formed a sort of "pillow" and he slept with his head against it, propped up rather high. More than once we have heard Groany snore, but Mimi was evidently too much of a lady.

When they felt chilly they covered themselves and the tops of their bowls, making their blankets as smooth as if rolled with a rolling pin. Lying on his back, Groany would stretch and smooth the pieces of terry cloth entirely across himself and over his bowl, working from underneath with both hands and feet. Mimi did the same. They often slept under a heap of blankets, and why they did not smother was a mystery. However, they were not content merely to sleep between layers of covers. Instead, they formed the middle layers into a neat little nest in which to curl up, as symmetrical and incredible as the neatest bird's nest. Mimi was the best nest-maker of the three, probably because she was a female, and her little sleeping chambers were always as round and smooth as if hollowed-out with an ice-cream dipper.

They were excellent barometers, as they always built their nests up high, with many blankets, before a storm or some other unpleasant change in the weather, a woods-animal instinct. Before the days of weather forecasts and storm warnings, when a farmer's very survival depended upon his knowledge of valid weather signs, many of his conclusions were based upon animal behavior and nature warnings. In the back country, these were known even to small children.

When bats fly low, it will rain soon. Insects on which the bats feed are forced down by the low air pressure before a rain, and the bats must fly low to catch them.

Red morning, take warning. This bit of weather wisdom is very old, and can be found in Matthew 16:3: "And in the morning, it will be foul weather today: for the sky is red and lowering."

When the smells from creeks, ponds, and swamps become stronger, there is stormy weather ahead. If the air pressure is high, these smells are held captive. When a low approaches, they are released.

When bees stay near the hive, rain is coming soon. It is axiomatic in back-country Indiana that a bee is never caught in a shower.

When spiders desert their webs, it will rain. The sight of insects seeking shelter is a very old portent of coming showers.

When drops hang suspended from fences or branches after a shower, the rain is not over, but will continue. These are not raindrops, but a condensation of moisture brought about by the contrasting temperatures of air and earth. They indicate the saturated atmosphere in which rain occurs.

If the sun should set in gray, the next will be a rainy day. Conversely, a red sunset meant fair weather ahead.

When the grass is dry on a summer night, look for rain. Dew is favored by cloudless skies and fair weather to come.

Spider webs shining early in the morning mean a fair day ahead. Spider webs in the grass are seldom noticed unless the dew is on them, and dew means good weather, fair skies, no wind.

Smoke falling instead of rising is a sign of bad weather. Smoke is carried toward the ground by the low air pressure before a rain or storm.

Look for rain when the trees turn their leaves upward, especially cottonwood trees. This is also said of grapevines.

1. Bill.

2. Groany, Mimi, and Shad as babies. Groany is still too young to sit up. *(Photo by Fred Lord)*

3. A week later: Mimi, Groany, and Shad. Groany sat up to eat for the first time.

4. Mimi and Groany when still very young. *(Photos by Fred Lord)*

5. Shad in the Mexican bean pot. *(Photo by Fred Lord)*

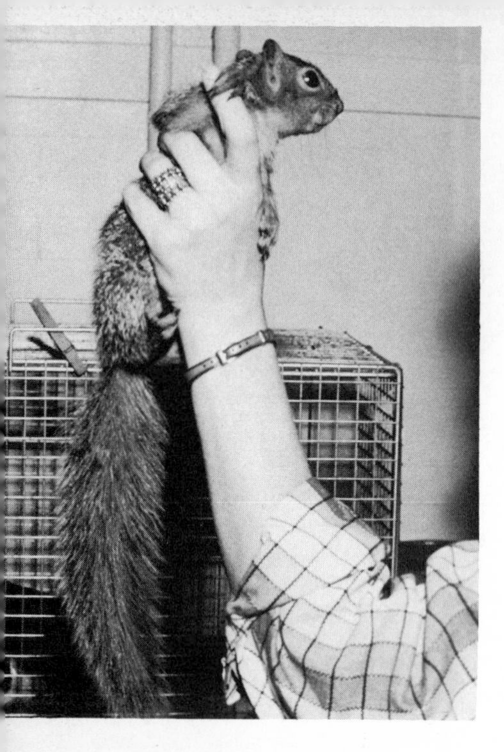

6. This shows how tiny Mimi was. *(Photo by Fred Lord)*

7. On a hot summer day, Groany liked to rest on a cool surface. *(Photo by Fred J. Miller)*

8. Mimi enjoying her favorite summer food, watermelon.

9. Groany would stop in the middle of lunch and hold up one arm to be scratched. *(Photos by Fred J. Miller)*

10. Groany wearing his winter fat . . .

11. . . . and taking grapes from my hand. *(Photos by Fred J. Miller)*

12. Chip-Chip when a baby. *(Photo by Fred J. Miller)*

13. Squirrels often rest with their arms around a branch. *(Photo by Karl Maslowski)*

14. Hands clasped in an "alarm" or "listening" pose.
(Photo by Karl Maslowski)

15. Chip-Chip, technical adviser.
(Photo by Lloyd Beesley)

All sorts of creatures and most people are ill-at-ease before a storm, with a strange restlessness they cannot explain. This is due, scientists tell us, to the many depressing and disturbing effects, both mental and physical, caused by low air pressure.

Such restlessness, noted by weather watchers for many, many years, is probably responsible for such observations as: *Before a storm, pigs squeal more than usual . . . frogs croak more rapidly . . . goats bleat a great deal . . . ducks quack noisily . . . horses stamp, switch their tails, and blow loudly, even when sheltered from flies . . . cows thump their ribs with their tails . . . crows caw more often . . . dogs are uneasy and keep changing positions . . . sheep huddle together . . . donkeys scratch themselves against walls and fences . . . fireflies wink faster . . . people may seem unnerved.* (Ella, my grandmother's "hired girl," used to say, "If it doesn't start raining pretty soon, I'll fly to pieces!")

One evening my brother-in-law, who pilots his own plane, was worrying about a business trip.

"I wish there was some way to know about tomorrow," he kept saying. "If it's going to be bad flying weather and I can't go, there are some things that ought to be done here, and I'd like to make plans. But the field only gives weather forecasts six hours in advance."

"Poor man," I said. "You are trapped by the age of automation. But there's a way out. Come and see."

I took him out of doors and showed him that the summer grass was covered with a heavy dew.

"That means tomorrow will be fair, so stop worrying. You can fly."

He was quite excited.

"How long has this system been used?" he asked. "Do the weather forecasters know about it?"

I said it had been known to some people since very early times. The Old Testament, in fact, tells how Gideon chose, for making war against the fierce desert Midianites, a day when "there was dew on all the ground." (Judges 6:40) And a very old weather rhyme declares:

When the dew is on the grass
Rain will never come to pass.

As for the forecasters, I had once asked the opinion of Tony Sands, well-known Cincinnati meteorologist, and he said 90 percent of the time would find truth in this folk legend.

"Few forecasters are more accurate than *that*," I added. It was accurate this time, too, and the next day my brother-in-law had a fair morning in which to take off.

One of the most interesting and accurate weather signs I learned from a retarded pupil in our back-country school, a twelve-year-old boy who could not learn, but who was sent to school anyway, and who was often taunted and ridiculed by other boys. In rural communities years ago (and in a few today) such a boy was known as the "village idiot" and made the butt of many heartless jokes, some perpetrated by "adults." Like other boys of such places and afflictions, this one spent many hours alone, away from the cruelty of his kind, found companionship in woods and hills, and developed a sure, almost uncanny knowledge of the wilds.

One day at school the boy stated quite innocently that the trees talked to him, which brought a howl of laughter from the other pupils. Shamed and bewildered, he ran out of the room to hide himself. I felt sorry for him and followed him and asked him, very respectfully, to tell me what the trees said. He did, and I listened and heard them saying it, and have heard them saying it ever since. "*Sh-h-h-h-h-h, rain. Sh-h-h-h-h, rain. Sh-h-h-h-h* . . ."

This is not a mere rustling of leaves, but a very special and unusual stirring, low and unbroken, which occurs some hours before a storm. And when I hear the trees talking, in the woods, along the street, or on a country road, I know rain is not far away. It was interesting to me to find that Bill, too, was aware of this special sound as a portent of rain, and he told me hunters said it was caused by "leaves trying to turn over."

On summer nights when a storm is gathering, when the air is hot and oppressive and thunder mutters in the distance, many little wild creatures can be seen feeding and foraging hurriedly, as though in anticipation of a time of hunger inside their nests and holes and burrows.

Squirrel nests, in summer, must be prepared for coming storms, made strong enough to turn rain and resist wind. However, all sorts of little woods creatures are destroyed in such storms and many times, when the trees were lashed mercilessly by wind and rain, I have heard birds crying out in helpless terror.

Squirrels avoid weather extremes, and no experienced or able hunter would look for fox squirrels on extremely hot or windy days. In winter they remain where it is dry and warm, avoiding foraging trips in snow, sleet, or blizzard unless desperate with hunger, waiting for the sun to come out and the days to grow warmer.

There were many dark winter days when Groany and Mimi didn't even get up, but spent the time lying quietly in their bowls, taking little naps, waking up again. Mimi might be awake for hours, looking solemn and meditative, often with one small hand clutching the rim of her bowl. When Groany was little, he would pass the time lying on his back and playing with his feet, like a baby. Both nibbled at snacks hidden in their blankets, especially Groany, who loved to eat in bed. Many times we have stood beside his bowl at night and heard a steady *crunch-crunch* from under his covers.

The "falling weather" (as Indiana hunters call it) that keeps squirrels inactive includes rain, sleet, fog, snow, mist, drizzle. Even on cloudy days they may remain hidden and half asleep. Ours were so quiet it was hard to believe they were really in the bowls, which seemed completely empty except for the blankets. But if we looked carefully, we could see that somewhere there was *always* a convenient peephole and one wary little eye looking out. (When we sat down in the woods to rest, Bill used to grin and say, "Wonder how many little fellers is watching us now?")

Contrary to what most people believe, woods animals are *not* impervious to winter winds and cold. If they venture out of their warm, dry homes and become wet or chilled, they may suffer colds, fever, even pneumonia.

That year, around Thanksgiving time, we had some warm and beautiful days, and I let Mimi play in an open window. Suddenly some clouds came up, the wind changed, and the air grew cold. I saw Mimi shiver violently, so I snatched her up and closed the window, but she became ill anyway.

Soon afterward I noticed that she stayed in her bowl, even though the day was sunny and bright. Also, she kept her head down, which (we learned later) is a symptom of headache in many animals. She ate nothing, and that evening her nose began to bleed and her breathing sounded unnatural. Our veterinarian was away, so I called another one, who said to bring her to his office at once and he would give her an antibiotic shot.

We wrapped her warmly in a blanket and put her in a covered basket. Apparently, very little is known about caring for sick squirrels, and the doctor said that he could only guess as to proper medication and dosage; but she would probably die without a shot, and so he gave her one. A squirrel's hide is extremely tough, not easy for a needle to penetrate, and Mimi cried a little, but did not go into shock as I had feared, probably because Lee was holding her.

The doctor said she had pneumonia, and when we brought her home, she was breathing with even greater difficulty. We did not put her back in the lamp bowl, but laid her in a comfortable basket filled with terry blankets and covered her warmly. Jamie and I watched over her all night.

Watching and nursing Mimi taught me a great deal about the symptoms of illness in a squirrel. When really sick, they feel hot, will not eat, and may or may not drink. If they have a fever, their noses seem hot and dry and they show a desire for water which is very unnatural.

They sit hunched forward with their heads lowered and their ears laid back instead of standing up. Their coats look rough instead of sleek; the fur seems to separate, and if they have much fever, will brush out when they are touched. Serious symptom: they cease to groom their tails.

I was awake a long time, lying on the sofa under an afghan, listening to the piteous sound of Mimi's hard, rasping breathing. Toward morning I dozed, and when I awoke again, there was no sound from the basket. I thought, with sinking heart: *Little Mimi is dead. . . .* But when I lifted the top blanket, she moved and looked up, weak and very sick, but alive and glad to see me. The basket was unfamiliar, and squirrels, if not frightened, are at least ill-at-ease in unfamiliar surroundings.

Jamie woke up, and Lee, and we all talked to Mimi and petted her, relieved that her breathing was more normal and she seemed better. Still, it was plain that she was seriously ill and might not recover. Her eyes were almost glazed; she was very hot, lapped a great deal of water, and would eat nothing.

Days passed. She seemed no better, became shockingly thin, and was so weak she could not stand without trembling all over. Excessive water made her kidneys more active, but she would not befoul her blankets. Desperately, with terrible weakness, she would scratch and scramble, trying to get out of the basket, and we would lift her out on a paper. The fever had affected her fur and it flew from her like dust when she moved.

We gave her round-the-clock nursing care. One of us stayed with her every moment. We brought her cool water, made up her bed with fresh blankets, kept her warm by putting hot-water bottles (tepid) near her basket. She seemed terribly afraid and was comforted when we talked to her and petted her.

Obviously she was too weak to eat, yet the lack of food was making her weaker. Finally, Lee brought home some jars of baby food and we fed it to her whenever she would take it, on the end of a spoon. She had always loved pears and liked baby-food pears because they were in the form of a sauce easy to eat and cooling to the tongue. She ate applesauce, too, and later ate some mashed squash and carrots, but preferred the pears.

Finally, the fever left her and she began to seem stronger. She drank less and ate more, which was a heartening sign. We gave her bits of cereal, scraped apple, some solid fruits and vegetables, and at last a few sunflower seeds and nut meats.

At night Lee carried her into the bedroom and let her lie beside him while he read. This pleased her so much that she had no desire to sleep elsewhere, and protested indignantly when we returned her to her basket.

As soon as she went back to grooming her tail, showing her saucy temper, and being curious about what was going on, we decided she was well again, even though she was still weak and thin. I observed, however, that there was something unnatural about her mouth. Lee opened it and looked in it. Her upper front teeth were gone! Apparently the severe infection she suffered had impaired and loosened them; they had come out of their sockets and gone, unnoticed, into a wastebasket when I shook out her blankets. She could no longer crack sunflower seeds and Lee had to open them for her.

People who observe fox squirrels closely over a period of time are always impressed by their affection for one another. Old hunters say that even after the mother leaves the den (they believe it is she who leaves, not the young squirrels), she does not forget them, but returns again and again to pay them little visits. People who had raised full litters (usually three babies) said that as long as the squirrels were kept together, they shared a close and tender companionship, but once they were separated for any length of time, this association was never wholly renewed.

Unlike animals that seem to take no notice of a companion's absence or death, Mimi had plainly missed Shad. While she was ill with pneumonia, Groany missed her in the same way, looked for her everywhere, even climbed up and peered into her bowl, trying to find her. For months they had romped and played together, sat side by side watching TV and listening to music, rolled and tumbled in mock quarrels and joyous games.

During the time Mimi was sick, however, this happy relationship was broken. When she was well again and we put her in Groany's cage, he ran to meet her with obvious delight, but she shrank away from him, filled with mistrust and apprehension. She hid from him, ran from him, scolded him when he came near. No doubt the fact that she was approaching her first mating season had much to do with her rejection of him, for squirrels seldom mate in captivity. But she never again went into the same cage with him, and though they played together at times and seemed to "talk" a great deal, they were never as close as before her illness. It was something Mr. Battles could never understand, for his squirrels, Mickey and Dickey, had lived in the same cage all their lives, slept in the same box, apparently with no loss during their lifetime of the trusting and childlike companionship they had shared since babyhood.

With each day, Mimi became more and more devoted to Lee. She would run to meet him when he came home in the evening, ride around on his shoulder, lie on the arm of his chair when he read the paper, sit on his knee while he cracked her sunflower seeds and fed them to her.

After dinner they had an hour's romp together, while Lee

sat on the floor and Mimi ran, leaped, jumped, rolled, bounced, and danced around and upon him, in a game somewhat like tag. Then if he watched the TV, she watched too, curled up in his lap. When he went to bed, she went along, waiting for her bedtime snack. Every evening Lee prepared some little tidbit for her (a nut, a grape, perhaps a piece of apple), put it in an ashtray, and slipped it into the top drawer of the bedside table. Instead of giving it to her at once, he waited until she "asked" for it. This she did by drawing close, with little *mm . . . mm* sounds, looking at him appealingly, leaning down and pointedly sniffing the drawer.

Even after she had eaten her evening treat (sitting up on the bedside table like a stuffed toy) she did not want to go back to her bowl. Instead, she wanted to sleep in Lee's bed.

People who write about wild-animal pets often mention that they develop a great liking for the comfortable beds of their owners. Mimi did, and being an extremely stubborn little creature, was determined to sleep there, by fair means or foul. During the day, when I found her bowl empty, I would go into the bedroom and see a little round lump in the very middle of the bed, under the quilt and bedspread, and between the sheets. This was Mimi, curled up and taking her siesta, and defying anyone to remove her from the warmest and cosiest nest she had ever found.

VIII

One of the best ways to learn how to care for a wild pet is to find, if possible, someone who has been successful in raising, feeding, taming, and training one like yours, then combine the fruits of this person's experience with the advice of veterinarians and naturalists.

A friend told me about a young secretary named Vera who had rescued and was bringing up a little fox squirrel and simply adored him.

"Personally, I think she's a little balmy about him," said my informant frankly.

This made Vera sound like an authority, so I contacted her, and like all owners of pet squirrels, we established an immediate rapport. I told her about Mimi and Groany, and she told me about Bushy. We visited each other's pets, and after that, whenever Lee and I had to be out of town, Vera took charge of our little ones as their official and executive squirrel-sitter.

About a year before I met Vera, she had been sitting in her living room, busy with some letters, when she heard a child's voice shouting, "*Kill it! Kill it!*" She looked out in time to see several boys and girls chasing something with sticks. One little girl made a grab at the earth and came up clutching a baby squirrel. Just at that moment, she tripped over some stones and fell, and the little animal escaped.

Vera, long a defender of pets wild and domestic, went to the door to see what had happened to him, and found him crouched in one corner of her porch, panting with terror, and utterly exhausted. When she went toward him, he could only stare at her pitifully, too spent to run any more.

She brought a little box and gently slipped him into it, then put it (covered) into a dark and quiet place. When the little squirrel had had time to rest and recover from his fright, she gave him food and water, talked to him soothingly. Each day he came closer to her, trusted her a little more. By gradual stages, he ate from her hand, climbed into her lap, nestled in her hand, and allowed her to pet him.

Because of his plumy tail, she named him Bushy. When she was able to examine him a little more closely, she saw that he had no broken bones (as she had feared) but he showed the effects of his hard fall upon the stones just the same. Evidently he had struck one of them with his chin, which was now bare of all fur and was marked by a blood-streaked abrasion.

Bushy became Vera's favorite pet and they shared the same sort of relationship that existed between Groany and me. He thought she was his mother. He was full of excitement when she came home at night, leaping upon her shoulder, nuzzling her neck, "talking" with the ecstatic sort of *mm . . . mm . . . mm*'s which greeted her in the morning. He was never ill, ate heartily, and played endlessly, skipping, hopping, twisting, bouncing. When she sat down to read, he curled up in the chair with her, and often slept with his head on her knee.

Bushy did not look a great deal like either of our squirrels, however. He was longer, more slender in build, and browner in color the year round. Now that Groany was older, his little white socks and vest had disappeared, and his feet and hands and tummy had become a soft beige, contrasting sharply with the rich fawn coat he wore on his back in the spring. But Mimi was always tawny-bright, and almost flame-colored in the fall. Both our squirrels were short, and built like little stuffed toys.

That year, when April came, we discovered that our little pets loved fragrant smells. It was enchanting to see Mimi sitting up with a violet in her tiny hands, smelling it happily, and to think of the wild squirrels smelling the woods flowers in the spring. Our squirrels loved roses, too, and not only smelled them but ate the petals, as Bill had described. I often brought them rose petals as a special treat. Once, in a farm store, I heard an elderly man say to his wife, "No, I'm not putting out any more roses! The squirrels will just come and eat the blooms!" His wife, who listened with an air of patient suffering, replied coldly, "Don't be ridiculous! Squirrels eat *nuts*, not tea roses!" (Madam, they enjoy both!) Mimi not only liked to smell flowers, but loved to parade around my dressing table sniffing cologne bottles, and Groany sometimes did this, too.

When the squirrels were little, we served their meals in ashtrays, but when they grew older and ate more, they had their food from plates which often appeared to be filled with delicious salads. There might be a vegetable plate with one slice each of cucumber, tomato, lettuce, butternut squash, and carrot, plus one green bean.

A fruit plate might contain a raspberry or strawberry, a small slice of fresh peach, watermelon, apple, pear, or plum, and two or three white grapes. At another time the plate might hold a few sunflower seeds, a pecan, hickory nut or walnut (the meat), perhaps an acorn or half a boiled chestnut, some rose petals, or a pink clover blossom.

They had their own food preferences, however. Mimi preferred a crisp lettuce leaf, but Groany wanted the lettuce heart, and had he known about ambrosia fit for the gods, this is how he would have classified it. Whenever I cut the heart out of a lettuce head, he bounced with joyful anticipation and could hardly wait to snatch it from me. Mimi cared little for carrots, but Groany loved them. Mimi ate a slice of apple every day; Groany ate one only occasionally. I have heard of pet squirrels who liked a bite of banana now and then, but ours refused it haughtily. (Too *messy!*)

Their natural appetites appeared to follow the seasons. They would not eat strawberries in December, though they loved them in May, nor watermelon in spring, no matter how high their regard for it in fall. We fed them only foods that were natural to them, and never allowed them to have the sort of bizarre "treats" that people sometimes inflict upon pets, things like ice cream, Danish pastry, and waffles.

In spring and summer, squirrels living out-of-doors eat wild strawberries, mulberries, raspberries, blackberries, dewberries, blueberries, and wild cherries. (Many times I have seen a squirrel sitting, bandy-legged, in a raspberry bush, stuffing himself with the tasty ripe fruit, his face and hands and feet stained purple. Probably their thick fur and tough hide protect them from the thorns.)

In the fall they reap a rich harvest of wild grapes, papaws, rose hips, wild plums and haw apples, wild persimmons, and all sorts of nuts. Indiana squirrels feast upon acorns (Groany almost swooned over them), hickory nuts, walnuts, butternuts, and beechnuts in years when the trees are bearing), but not buckeyes, which are poison.

In orchards and fields they help themselves to small portions of melon, squash, pumpkin, tomato, apples, peaches, and pears. Pears, nuts, and corn are probably their favorite autumn foods, and though they eat corn from the green season through the dry, the amount they take is negligible. In pioneer days, however, when it was a terrible effort to provide enough corn for even a small family, such pilfering by squirrels was a very serious matter.

Groany was as meticulous about food as about everything else, and would eat it only when it was perfectly sound and fresh. Mimi, on the other hand, often buried pieces of sound and fresh food in her bowl, and ate them only after they became a little "gamy." We were always searching out and removing such cherished tidbits as a slightly damaged piece of peach, an old pecan, or a withered grape.

Neither of our squirrels liked parsley, and as for cabbage, parsnips, and turnips, they would not even *smell* them except in horror. We sometimes gave them freshly washed mulberry leaves, but were very cautious about allowing them to have bark or foliage of any kind, always first checking with authorities, since so many leaves are poison, as are some kinds of bark.

Due to the loss of her front teeth, Mimi ate with a good deal of difficulty at times. Lee opened sunflower seeds for her and we shredded such vegetables as carrots, which she sometimes wanted but could not bite. However, she became quite skilled at eating with only her lower teeth, would hold half an unshelled English walnut in her hands, as if holding a tiny bowl, and scoop out the meat. She loved chestnuts and could eat them in the same fashion if we boiled them a little and then cut them in two. And she could scrape apple out of the skin. When Lee was away, she managed very well by herself, but when he was at home, she sat pitifully on his knee and waited for him to feed her.

Groany's teeth were in perfect condition, but he never learned to open a nut. He would spend all day on a black walnut, grinding, cutting, working like a little galley slave, but the most he ever accomplished was a small hole in the wrong place.

"I'm sorry you have such an ignorant mother," I would tell him, "but I can't help you a bit."

Both Mimi and Groany drank a good deal of water in late winter and early spring, as the mating seasons approached. Groany soon learned where water was to be found, and would go to the sink and stand with his hands on the base-cabinet below it, like a puppy asking for a drink. Mimi would turn to one of us and chatter demandingly.

Later, Groany learned to drink while standing on the porcelain divider of the double sink, catching the water as it flowed from the tap. He always preferred running water. Mimi, on the other hand, drank from her little cup (a doll cup), lapping the water like a kitten as we held it to her lips. Of course, drinking wet their whiskers, which both found highly objectionable, though Mimi was never as upset about it as Groany. They would immediately wipe their mouths on whatever was handy, often on our sleeves.

We had a birdbath under a tree near the kitchen window, and I have seen the wild squirrels drink from it many times. A squirrel, after looking carefully around, would slowly descend the tree and lap some water from the bowl while hanging from the bark by his back feet. He then hurried up to one of the forks, where he sat down and wiped his mouth on a branch, just as Mimi and Groany wiped *their* mouths, as promptly as possible.

Squirrels seldom drink and apparently get most of their moisture from fruits and vegetables. Hunters never expect to find them at streams, ponds, or creeks, but Bill had showed me squirrels licking dew from the leaves in early morning, raindrops from leaves after a summer shower, holding a chunk of snow in their little hands and eating it as though it were an ice-cream cone. He said he had seen squirrels drink from grass-pools or puddles once or twice, after a rain, but I have met hunters who said they never in all their lives saw a squirrel drink anything.

During the terrible drought of 1935, squirrels were observed moving into the vicinity of streams, lakes, and ponds, which was very unusual, as normally they make no special effort to den near water. In the same year Bill saw a migration of squirrels swimming the Ohio. Squirrels are good swimmers, he always told me, but during large movements of this kind, many are lost through drowning or exhaustion. I never saw a squirrel swim, but he said they swim easily, holding their tails high, for an upright tail can serve as a rudder, but a drenched tail will drag them under and drown them.

Mimi and Groany sometimes drank a little fruit juice, and Groany loved watermelon juice. Mimi had a perfect passion for Coca-Cola, which she first tasted by accident. After that, she would identify it by smell when Lee drank it, and beg for it until he poured some into her cup for her. On very hot days, both squirrels would lick ice cubes, but might go for weeks without drinking at all. We offered them water almost as regularly as we offered them food, but they refused it except during very hot weather, or when they were nearing the mating season.

In spring, after the snow had melted, I observed that the outside squirrels were busily digging up nuts, and just as busily snipping buds from the trees. In the woods they eat certain plants and shoots and roots dug out of the soil which we were unable to identify.

Naturalists say that squirrels will eat insects, especially when other food is scarce, sometimes digging or flushing them out from under bark and leaves in wintertime. I never witnessed this, but Jamie said she saw Mimi snatch up and eat a spider, and Bill had seen squirrels eat beetles and moths.

It is persistently alleged that squirrels eat birds' eggs, but for a long time I did not believe this at all. I thought perhaps they stole eggs, not because they wanted to eat them, but because they will take anything egg-shaped, evidently thinking it a nut. I was never able to persuade either Mimi or Groany to eat or even taste a cooked egg of any kind, and as for raw eggs . . . *heaven forbid!* What could be more *sticky?*

In the wilds, squirrels nibble the seeds of grains and grasses, and seem to have a great fondness for them. One day I heard shrill cries of terror from Pete, our yellow canary, and when I rushed to his rescue, found Mimi sitting on top of his cage with his treat cup clutched in both her hands. She had yanked if off the cage herself, and was calmly licking the last of the seeds from it.

We gave her some birdseed several times after that, but she didn't want it as a gift, she wanted to steal it. She would watch her chance, snatch the treat cup, and run with it, spilling seed all the way. It is not surprising that Pete was terrified, for she must have looked as large as a Kodiak bear to him. But after a while he became quite accustomed to her mischief, and when she leaped upon his cage and took his treat, he did not even stop singing.

Everyone who knows anything at all about squirrels is profoundly impressed by their incredibly acute sense of smell. Bill maintained that hunters were stupid to smoke in the woods, saying that the smell of tobacco was associated with man, and therefore a warning to all game animals, especially squirrels, who could detect the smallest whiff at some distance.

Groany's remarkable sense of smell was demonstrated more than once in connection with fresh cucumbers. I allowed him to eat only one or two slices at a time, as I thought more might be injurious to him. But if he knew I *had* any more, he would make a terrible fuss, trying to get into the refrigerator, or perhaps running up and down his cage, banging and clanging.

One afternoon, when he was asleep, I tiptoed to the refrigerator and silently removed a cucumber. Then, because I didn't want him to have any of it, I tiptoed past him, going into the pantry—but it was no use. Even in a sound sleep, he smelled the cucumber and shot up, wide awake, his nose twitching.

Lee came in one night with a large bag of food items, including a box of peanut brittle. Almost before the bag was on the counter top, Groany leaped to it, unerringly ripped it open at the very spot where the box was concealed, and just as swiftly and unerringly slashed the box, jerking out a piece of the nut candy. This was done in a flash, really before we could stop him.

At breakfast Lee very often ate cornflakes. Squirrels are attracted by any smell of corn, so Groany would climb upon his knee and steal a cornflake from his bowl. Nearly every morning they had breakfast together. Two or three pilfered flakes were quite enough for Groany, who held them in his little hands, one at a time, and nibbled them fondly. (Mimi's favorite breakfast: one grape.)

But, if the cornflakes were not Kellogg's, Groany would scorn them. We tried all the different brands, but could never fool him. He detected Kellogg's instantly, by his superior sense of smell, and would eat no other kind, regardless of how appetizing they might look.

Visitors were always fascinated by our pets, and usually insulted by them. When strangers appeared, both Mimi and Groany would dive into their bowls and cover up, Mimi often screaming in inhospitable rage.

If they were not close to their bowls, or to any other convenient hiding place at the time, they would conceal themselves behind us, or perhaps just rudely (and pointedly) turn their backs. However, neither showed any apprehension when approached for the first time by Lee's brother or my sister, which suggested that they might carry a "family smell" which held no terrors for our squirrels.

Since both Groany and Mimi were afraid of bright lights, it was very difficult to photograph them. Mimi quickly learned to recognize my camera, and would hide when she saw me coming with it.

Perhaps it was the lightning which caused them to fear thunderstorms. Once, in the night, when there was a crash of thunder and a blinding flash, I saw Mimi standing up in her lamp bowl, her little hands fighting frantically to pull a drapery over her head. After that, when we had storms at night, Lee would get up to comfort her, and often took her back to bed with him, where she slept under the covers at his feet, safe from all alarms.

As they grew older, the squirrels ceased to purr when petted, but talked in variations of the *mm . . . mm . . . mm* sounds, a kind of soft burbling. Mimi even managed to tell Lee when I had spanked her for being naughty. The moment he came in, she would run to him, leap to his shoulder, and "talk" in a rapid, excited earnest manner reserved for these occasions, "*Mmmmmm . . . mm . . . mmm . . . mmmmm-mmmmmmmm!*" which was not unlike the sound of an eccentric percolator. Lee, taking up for her, would immediately demand, "What have you been doing to my little squirrel?"

Groany was always sweet and obedient and never got into the sort of mischief that was Mimi's chief joy in life, but as he grew older, he developed a temper of no small proportions. Once, when I had a fly swatter in my hand, I playfully swatted him, and he seemed to think the swatter was some new and dangerous enemy. With a snarl (he snarled like a dog when angry, even curling his upper lip), he charged it, leaping with all four feet close together, claws curved and spread wide, teeth bared. With such weapons he could undoubtedly inflict some painful wounds, even disembowel a small animal, for despite their size, squirrels are surprisingly strong. I have seen a small squirrel leap from branch to branch, carrying a whole ear of corn. Once, when Lee laid down a large and heavy hammer, Groany went up to it, slid his teeth along the handle, quickly located the center of balance, picked the hammer up in his mouth, and walked away with it.

Mimi had a pert temper of her own. When I told her to leave some particular object alone, she would stare at me with unmistakable insolence, and if I picked her up to remove her from temptation, she would promptly slash me with her back feet. After being slashed once or twice in this fashion, I approached her (in matters of discipline) only when I was wearing a heavy jacket or shirt, for her strong feet and sharp claws inflicted terrible gashes on my arms. A savage lashing out with the back feet seems to be the female's method of fighting, and a pretty effective one.

Sometimes, when angry, she would catch my hand in her mouth, as if to bite through the soft part of my palm. I was not much afraid of this, since she had no upper teeth, and anyway I don't think she really meant to bite me. She would seize my hand in her mouth and just stare at me, as though to show me what she could do if she wished. Lee thought this adorable.

One warm and rainy spring day Groany stayed in his bowl and napped, as he did on all rainy days, but for some reason, Mimi decided to get out and play. I let her play in our bedroom because I was cleaning the kitchen and going in and out a great deal, and didn't want to take the time to watch her.

Both squirrels loved to play on the bed, and would skip, hop, jump, caper, and romp on this pleasant surface. One of Groany's favorite pastimes was to run as fast as he could go, around and around and around the foot of a Hollywood bed, across the dust ruffle at the front, then up and across the foot and back down across the dust ruffle, perhaps as many as ten times before he rested. I have seen squirrels fleeing in the woods many times and have been astonished by their speed, but never saw one that could compare to Groany. When he came to me afterward and put his head near my lips for me to whisper to him, as he so often did, I would say, "Incontestably and indubitably, you are the fastest squirrel in the world!" I have read that fox squirrels can travel fifteen miles an hour, and am sure Groany went faster.

Mimi, too, was very fast on her feet, especially when being naughty. If she was not supposed to go into the living room, that was exactly where she would be found. The moment she heard somebody open the French doors, she was off like a shot to get through them, always starting her effort with a tremendous leap, as much as ten feet.

The rainy afternoon when I thought her safely in the bedroom, Lee came home and said she wasn't there. We called her, but she did not come, which was unusual indeed. We looked under the bed, behind the pillows, back of the chairs, in every corner, but Mimi was not to be found. Lee was as agitated as a hen who has lost her only chick.

"Where did you leave her?" he kept demanding, as though I had plotted the whole thing. "What did you do with her? Where did you see her last? How could she get out of this room?" Which was a mystery, as the windows were closed and the door, too, though I had opened it several times, going in and out.

We hunted for more than an hour. We searched the closet, looking in boxes (she was adept at removing lids), behind hangers full of clothes, even in Lee's loafers and house shoes. Then we abandoned the bedroom and hunted through the other rooms, calling and searching. Jamie, who was upstairs, came down to join the hunt.

"She just isn't in here," said Lee at last. "Somehow or other, she must have slipped past you when you went out on the porch. . . ."

"I think so, too," agreed Jamie. "I'll go out and look for her. She may be in one of the trees."

The thought of Mimi, alone and frightened, out in the cold rain, sent Lee into a near tizzy, but did not impress me at all.

"I don't believe it," I said flatly. "Mimi may be sly and smart, but I have a *little* sense of my own, and I'm sure I'd have caught her slipping past me."

"You know how quick she is," Lee reminded me, sadly.

"Still, I don't believe she ever got out of the bedroom."

Somewhat heartened, he began to search the closet again. He found no sign of her on shelf or floor, but as he pushed aside the hanger holding his topcoat, he noticed that one sleeve seemed oddly heavy. Reaching into it, he encountered a warm, soft, furry little body, and peeped in to find Mimi anchored there, fast asleep. Joyfully he woke her up and took her out, and petted and made a great fuss over her, much to her drowsy surprise, I think.

Mimi was the softest and prettiest little creature imaginable, except for her claws. Lee said she was like a powder puff with thorns. Groany, too, had terrible claws and often scratched me accidently when he hopped upon my shoulder or arm, so I insisted that we clip them. He made no fuss while we did this, but immediately afterward returned to his bowl and stayed there all day. When I peeped in at him, I found him busily at work nibbling the claws, making them needle-sharp again.

A little later that spring, a troubling change came over Mimi. She seemed to lose her zest for living, even abandoned her naughtiness and disobedience. It was as if her merry and insolent spirit had deserted her completely. She began to grow thin, stayed in her bowl a great deal, and would not eat no matter how tempting the tidbits Lee tried to feed her. During the day she was very quiet, and would try to avoid moving.

I told Lee I thought something was wrong with her mouth because she kept rubbing it against things, and I noticed that it seemed to hang open a little. Also, she kept holding her head down, as if to ease pain. Though she resisted a little this time, he finally persuaded her to let him look inside her mouth, and he was horrified by his discovery. Her lower teeth had kept on growing, with no upper teeth to correct them, and were so long that she was unable to eat or close her mouth properly. When she moved, these sharp lower incisors bit into her upper gums, which accounted for her being so quiet.

We called the veterinarian, and he said to bring her to the animal hospital and he would clip her teeth short. Since Shad's death, I had been terribly afraid of the squirrels' going into shock, but Lee said he thought she would be all right if he held her. She struggled a little when he laid her down on her back, for fox squirrels never like to expose their tender and vulnerable bellies to an enemy, but she gave up when she realized it was useless, and submitted with a pitiful little cry of despair. It took only a split second for the doctor to clip the extra growth from her lower incisors, and we measured the discarded pieces. They were more than half an inch long.

After that we had to take Mimi to the animal hospital every month to have her teeth clipped. She hated these trips, would hide when she saw her basket ready, struggle when we put her in it, and try to gnaw her way out as we drove along. When Lee put her down on her back (the best position for working on her mouth) she fought to turn over, an instinctive defense. When the doctor started to place the clippers, she would put out both little arms and try to hold him off. But at last, immoblized and somewhat soothed by Lee, she would give her little cry of defeat and let the doctor clip the teeth. Sometimes the trip was such an ordeal for her that she was completed disoriented when we got her home, and ran about in great panic and confusion, unable to find her bowl. Lee felt so sorry for her that he finally bought clippers of his own and clipped her teeth himself. He would tuck her in beside him at bedtime, wait until she was quite sleepy, then adjust the clippers and remove the tops of the teeth so gently and inoffensively that she hardly knew it.

Late in the summer Vera called me and said something was wrong with Bushy. He was too quiet, stayed in bed, and would not play or even eat, kept rubbing his face against things, acted sick, and kept his head down. With the air of an experienced veterinarian, I advised her to look in his mouth and, if possible, feel inside it.

When she did, she was as shocked as Lee had been. Evidently when the child had dropped him in his babyhood and Bushy had struck his little chin on the rock, he had dislocated his jaw, and this had resulted in a malocclusion. His upper teeth, not meeting his lower ones, had grown so long that they curled back into his mouth; they had kept on growing, and were now rubbing the roof of his mouth, making it extremely sore and painful. Gnawing animals who suffer such accidents in the wilds may die of starvation.

Because Vera had no car, we said we would drive her to the animal hospital, and I asked if she would like to borrow, to carry Bushy, the small closed basket which Lee always called "the Mimi toter."

"Oh, no," she said. "Thank you, but it won't be necessary. He won't cause any trouble. He's very good."

"But he's certain to be scared," I protested, "and may run around and bump into things and hurt himself."

"Oh, no," said Vera calmly. "I'll put him in a homemade strait jacket."

When we picked her up, she came running out carrying what looked like a sausage sack stuffed with a squirrel. She had made a little cloth tube with drawstrings at top and bottom, slipped Bushy into it, and pulled up the strings. His head protruded from the top, his tail waved from the other end. I was astounded.

"Doesn't he *mind?*" I asked, thinking he must be very sick indeed.

"As I said," Vera answered, "he's very docile."

This was another way in which he was quite different from our squirrels. He not only was built differently and had dissimilar coloring, he had a dissimilar temperament. Mimi or Groany would have fought to the death to escape from this sausage sack (if they could have been pushed into it at all), with screaming, squalling, biting, and slashing. They were very high-strung and I had never seen one of them really calm, for even when they lay quiet and apparently at ease, they were wary and on edge. Both would have died in restraint, I feel certain.

Bushy, however, seemed quite placid. He lay in Vera's arms

all the way, and though he had never before ridden in a car, it seemed to hold no terrors for him. When she placed him on the table under the veterinarian's astonished eyes (home-made strait jackets for animals were obviously new to him), Bushy made no move to resist. Vera opened his mouth, for he was as trusting toward her as Mimi was toward Lee; the doctor examined his mouth and looked rather startled.

Only when the doctor began to work with him and it pained him did Bushy cry out. Then he struggled so violently that it took both Vera and Lee to hold him still and keep him from rolling off the examination table. In a moment, though, the horribly curled incisors were cut.

Vera called me about three days later and said he had eaten some fruit and mashed nuts for the first time.

"When we came home, he still seemed to be in pain," she reported, "and would not open his mouth or try to eat until now. The whole thing must have been very painful for him, and I dread having to take him again."

As it happened, however, there was no need for her to go back. She found later that Bushy's desperate struggle on the examination table had corrected his dislocated jaw. From that day on, he had perfect occlusion, ate with ease, could gnaw all the walnut shells he wished, and never again had to have his teeth clipped.

Mimi began to molt in April that year, but Groany, for some unknown reason, did not molt until late in July. (The next year, both squirrels molted in the spring.)

Mimi's rather coarse "baby fur" now began to disappear from the top of her head and back of her neck, leaving beautiful new fur underneath. The old fur at her back then formed a V pointed toward her head. As it receded, the new fur appeared, finer, shinier. The last parts of her body to molt were her thighs.

One book about wildlife said that the spring molt begins on the head and spreads toward the tail, whereas the fall molt begins on the back and spreads in both directions. Another such book said the spring molt begins at the head, and the fall molt begins at the rump.

It is possible that a different subspecies might have a different pattern of molting, but insofar as *our* squirrels were concerned, the molts (usually April and September) *both* began at the head and proceeded to the tail. The tail molt seemed to start at the tip.

This process required about a month, during which time our pets became so thin that I was worried about them. One day when Mr. Dubbs stopped in to give me some more advice, I asked him anxiously, "Did your squirrels get thin when they molted?"

He considered this a long time, looking very thoughtful.

"Well, no," he answered at last, "can't say as they did." Then he brightened and added, "But they sure got thin when they shed!"

Squirrels are creatures of habit, and this characteristic is their strongest defense against their enemies. By following the same paths, trails, and routes they learn to know their home territory intimately, to know what food, water, and hiding places it provides.

Like the wild squirrels, Mimi and Groany had their chosen locations for eating, drinking, napping, resting, hiding, or play, all of which were done according to favored routines.

Mimi was now sleeping at Lee's feet every night, and had a routine for this, too. She would sit on his bedside table, eat her little snack, then slip down beside him to tell him goodnight. With her mouth close to his ear, she would murmur "*Mmmmmmmmmmmm* . . ." in tones of gentle affection. Then she would go on down to the foot of the bed and curl up for a good night's sleep, but first she would turn and look over at me and say, "*Kack!*" What this remark meant is uncertain, I am sure, but it had the sound of a sharp reprimand to a gross intruder.

IX Squirrels have many natural enemies in the woods, including the red-tailed hawk, a large and powerful predator that will swoop down and snatch a baby squirrel from a branch or kill its mother on the ground. It was because he terrorized and destroyed so many of my favorite woodland creatures that I disliked the red-tailed hawk, and very often sent one fleeing from the vicinity of a den tree with a bullet past his evil eye.

Indiana law protects this bold and handsome marauder (he destroys pests, too), and for this reason, Bill agreed that it would be most illegal to shoot him. I always suspected, however, that he was less law-abiding in this respect when I was not with him. Once, under a tree near his woods, I found a dead hawk with a wingspread of nearly four and a half feet and showed it to Bill. "*Poor* thing!" he said, shaking his grizzled head. "Some feller must of up and shot the varminty cuss!"

Red-tailed hawks kill large and small squirrels, large and small rabbits, skunks, meadow mice, pheasants, quail, toads, frogs, all kinds of poultry, and many smaller creatures. They are very arrogant and may become unbelievably bold. When I was a child and lived on a back-country farm, there was a red-tailed hawk that preyed constantly upon my grandmother's chickens. Apparently he had already had one narrow escape from an embattled farmer, for there was a large hole in his right wing where a bullet had knocked out the feathers and let in the daylight. He would sail above the farmhouse in slow and menacing circles, but if he came at noon when my grandfather was at home, he was courting disaster.

The moment his shadow fell upon the chickens, they set up a crying and fluttering of pure terror, like no other sound. "*The hawk!*" my grandmother would exclaim, and my grandfather would seize the shotgun and rush outside. But the moment my grandfather appeared, this wily old bird sailed out of range.

We wondered if he learned to fear a shotgun and sensed the time of day it was most likely to threaten him, as crows have been known to do. For after a while, he no longer came at noon, but only after my grandfather had returned to the fields.

Once when my grandmother was feeding some hens with chicks, the hawk dropped from the sky like a bullet, and seized a chick while so close to her feet that she flapped him with her apron. Again, when she saw him swooping down upon her chicks, she ran out and struck him with her broom, but he recovered his flight and rose in the air to return another day. (Marjorie told me she once heard a deputy sheriff say, "Wherever there's trouble, you'll find a woman with a broom!")

A certain Indiana wildlife bulletin says (and in a rather hurt manner, it seems to me) that "there has long been a deep-rooted and ineradicable prejudice in the minds of the general public . . . especially farmers . . . against all of our so-called birds of prey," which obviously includes the red-tailed hawk. I am sure my grandmother would have been happy to add her voice to this "ineradicable prejudice" and so would other people with a feeling for small rabbits, squirrels, skunks, meadow mice, pheasants, quail, and birds.

One of my friends, a naturalist, said to me, "About the

red-tailed hawk . . . you're prejudiced, too, you know. He's really a magnificent bird, fascinating to study, and when he makes a kill, it is only out of hunger. If he did *not* destroy the old and the sick and the weak, they would die a death far worse. As it is, they go into shock and expire immediately, and cannot be said to suffer."

It is difficult to accept this image of the red-tailed hawk, inasmuch as I have seen him snatch terrified babies away from their mothers, even out of their nests. To me, he seems less a magnificent bird than an arrogant outlaw. Yet I must admit being biased, for I admire crows, who sometimes do the same thing—though not, I think, with quite the same ruthlessness and frequency.

For a long time, the little creatures in Marjorie's woods were terrified by a red-tailed hawk that came shrieking over them several times a day. The moment his menacing shadow and whistling voice threatened them, they were instantly silent, instantly vanished into hidden retreats. Only the crows went up to meet him, for crows hate a red-tailed hawk with what resembles an ancient and hereditary hatred, will attack and drive him off with piercing cries of rage.

Marjorie most often observed this hawk as he was sitting on the topmost branch of a dead tree at the edge of the woods, surveying the landscape for prey. Once she saw him swoop to the ground with a rush of wings and rise again carrying a beautiful fox squirrel. Evidently the squirrel had been killed when the deadly talons pierced its body.

Foxes, too, prey upon squirrels. A hunter once told me that just as he shot a fox squirrel out of a walnut tree, a fox dashed from the underbrush, seized the animal, and fled with it. Squirrels are surrounded by enemies, and any female who makes her nest in a readily accessible place may find herself and her babies seized by a fox, hawk, raccoon, or owl.

When we read that squirrels have little to fear from owls because "squirrels are asleep in their dens when owls are feeding," we have wondered, and quite reasonably I think, if this is really true.

I have heard Bill say many times that night in the woods is "a diff'runt world," especially a bright summer night when there is a full moon. For the wild creatures, night begins with the fading of the sunset, when cardinals sing their evening songs, crows settle in their shabby nests, quail cease their bob-white calls, and nighthawks rise into the darkening skies. Then the bats come out of hidden places, the owls leave their nesting holes, fireflies rise above the wheat fields, and the last sound of the day is heard, the melancholy notes of the little peewee. Others must have thought, as I do, that his song is a sad one, for a poet, John Townsend Trowbridge, once wrote:

Hast thou, too, in thy little breast
Strange longings for a happier lot?

Many times when I and some of the members of my family were spending an evening with Bill, we would sit out under the trees near his flower garden and watch the moon come up, and talk about the woods at night and the little creatures that hunted there and were seldom seen in the light of day. It was late summer, usually, and there were crickets chirping in the grass, and a heady fragrance of apples and grapes on the air. Sometimes two or three of Bill's cronies would be there, and the talk was of wildlife and hunting, and old stories that dealt with strange happenings no man could explain. I would sit there in the soft darkness and look up at the stars and listen to the voices rising and falling, and think what wonderful experiences are lost to the young who find no companionship with the old, who neither savor their wisdom nor profit from their years.

One of their most fascinating stories (at least to me) was about three brothers, Dave and Ab and Jed, who lived in the hills of southern Indiana, and were three of the best shots in the state. Year after year they hunted together, from the time they was little fellers, till misfortune overtook them. Dave come down with a fever and died, and Ab was killed a year later by a falling tree, when he was lumbering. Jed, the youngest, outlived them by forty years, tramped the woods and hills alone, hunted alone, and done hisself proud, but seemed like he never had the same heart for it after his brothers was gone.

Finally Jed got old and sick and come to die, but he laid bedfast for many a week. His wife noticed that he got sort of be-addled toward the last, mumbled a lot, and didn't always know what was going on. But one day he seemed a lot clearer, and all of a sudden he told her, "Dave and Ab was here this morning, said their guns was outside and let's go hunting together. But I don't feel so good today; I'm still awful frail. So I told them to come back, five o'clock Wednesday, and I'd be ready, and we'd sure-enough go!"

His wife didn't pay any mind to such talk, but (I reckon you got it figured out by now) Jed died at five o'clock on Wednesday morning. And the last thing he said was, "Fetch me my twelve-gauge. They're here."

Sometimes, on evenings when the grass was dry, the bats would skim low and then the old hunters said rain was not far off, and talked with wonder about the ability of these little flying animals to avoid striking as much as a grapevine tendril, as they darted about.

Radar was then unknown, and none of us dreamed that bats have a built-in radar of their own, that their keen ears catch the echo of their own piping voices, a sound which is bounced off obstacles and reflected back to the bat, letting him know where the way is clear. Since his incessant piping is "supersonic" and therefore usually beyond our ears, it is seldom heard. On quiet nights, however, it is sometimes within our auditory range, especially when the bats are low and there is a storm brewing. I have heard the piping of bats many times in the silence of the back country, and Lee and I sometimes hear it outside our bedroom window when a midnight hush falls upon the streets of the town.

The men told how bats swoop down over ponds and lakes, scooping water into their mouths as they fly, sometimes being caught by a leaping fish—how their young ones (when babies) cling tight to their fur and ride along. But when these youngsters are older, heavier, and more likely to cause trouble, the mother just hangs them up in a safe place and leaves them there until she returns, a custom over which the men chuckled approvingly. Bill once knew a woman who had a pet bat (which sounded ghastly to me), but she said it was very docile, would come when she called it, and ate raw hamburger bits from her hand.

There was always talk about wild pets, for hunters often found orphaned animals in the woods, took them home, fed and cared for them. Most of them had owned a pet skunk, raccoon, or ground hog (woodchuck), perhaps a small chipmunk, squirrel, or possum, but nobody wanted a weasel, and they shot these bloodthirsty predators on sight. Most people who live in the back country have known a weasel to invade a chicken house at night, not to kill and eat one or two of the chickens, but to rush insanely about, slaughtering as many as possible, even while being pursued by an armed and shouting farmer.

The weasel is a crafty, vicious, and ferocious killer for which no good word can be said. He lopes as he travels, and there is a note shuddery and chilling in the very sound of his call, "Took-took-took-took!" as it echoes through the darkness.

The weasel hunts mostly after dark, will leap suddenly upon some prey such as a rabbit, fasten himself to its back, ride it, tumble and roll with it, as he struggles for the jugular vein. If the rabbit is lucky, the weasel is dislodged. If not, he bites through the vein with lightning swiftness and feeds upon the rabbit's flesh. When his prey is a very small bird or animal, he devours all of it, fur, feathers, and bone.

Another hunting animal quite as deadly as the weasel is the common house cat, one of the most vicious of all predators, even when he is a well-fed pet. He is able to climb the highest trees and, with his merciless front claws, rake whole families of sleeping baby birds and animals out of their nests. Permitting house cats to roam and hunt at will has been responsible for the wanton and senseless destruction of much valuable wildlife.

Though a cat may appear gentle, peaceful, and harmless while purring by his own fireside, once night falls and the moon rises he becomes, in the best tradition of the werewolf, another creature, vicious, savage, and cruel. Many cat lovers are almost unaware of this side of the animal's nature, and have never experienced (as I have) anything like a cat chasing a small chipmunk and biting off its head at such speed that the bloody and decapitated chipmunk kept on running.

Unwanted cats abandoned in the back country sometimes grow up in the woods, learn to live by hunting, and become half-wild animals enormous in size. Bill shot one on his creek bank one bright summer night, thinking it a roaming bobcat.

Watching along a stream on bright moonlit nights was one of Bill's favorite pastimes. He liked to see the coons come down on little feet that left tracks in the mud like tiny handprints, watch them feeling in the rocks for crawfish, scrubbing their food in the water, ambling off in search of beetles, insects, grubs, and fruit, especially persimmons. Coons love green corn, too, and sometimes it is provided especially for them. A farmer in the wooded hills of Franklin County once showed us a large cornfield and told us, "I planted the middle rows for myself. Those three outside rows around the field are for the coons."

Several of the men had owned pet coons, which they talked about with great tenderness and profound nostalgia. A coon, when little, is playful, affectionate, and easy to train, they said, but once he has reached the mating age, the voice of the wild is loud in his ears and will call him back to the woods forever, no matter how much he has loved his human friends and his first home. Coons are very intelligent animals, can use their clever little hands with great dexterity and ingenuity, and will play with toys like children. One man gave his pet coon the baby's rattle, which the little animal loved so much that he guarded it from seizure, played with it for hours, and refused to give it back.

Bill said the name "raccoon" comes from the Indian word *arakun*. ("Woodchuck" is said to have a similar origin, the Indian word *otchock*.) I have always thought baby coons adorable, and have seen them asleep many times on warm afternoons, totally oblivious to all about them, sometimes two or three curled up together. Once Lee and I saw a little coon sound asleep in a persimmon tree, his fat little tummy stuffed, no doubt, with this delicious fall fruit.

Skunks, the old men agreed, made gentle, playful, and affectionate pets, and it was funny to watch them growling and stamping their little feet when they were angry about something. But skunks never lived long in captivity, and it was best to set them free if you could. They were night feeders, eating grasshoppers, field mice, fruit, and other things, avoiding the sun, which could be very injurious to them. I was fascinated to hear that after the young ones are weaned, the mother hunts food and brings it back to the nest to them, as mother birds do.

Sometimes we saw a possum slipping down the meadow toward the red haw tree. Possums move so silently that you seldom knew they were near until you saw one passing, as white as a little ghost-animal in the moonlight. There are people who have rescued orphaned possums, tended and loved them, but the thought of a pet scavenger never appealed to me. Of course, they eat many things besides carrion—small animals, certain snakes, garden vegetables, birds, eggs, corn.

A possum is perhaps best known for his habit of "playing

dead" when overtaken by an enemy. When it was first reported, mostly by hunters and wildlife observers, that other animals also used this means of survival, the story was ridiculed and vehemently denied. Now it is an accepted fact, readily verified by naturalists, that many animals with no apparent means of escape will feign death, and by doing so, save themselves from predators seeking live prey. However, this is *not* a cleverly calculated ruse on the part of the animal, but a brief nervous collapse, nature's method of diverting his enemies and perhaps sparing his life.

Owls called through the woods and across the fields in the darkness and by moonlight—barn owls, barred owls, screech owls, and sometimes a great horned owl. Owl calls are easy to imitate, and in early Indiana were used as signals by hunting or marauding Indians.

There is an old superstition in the back country which says that hearing an owl call will bring you bad luck *unless* you put your shoes in a corner, which some people actually do. Another superstition declares that hearing an owl in the daytime, especially a barred owl, will bring misfortune, but some people deny this and say it will bring company instead. Bill never called a barred owl anything but an "eight owl," because of the eight notes in its call.

Frogs and toads added their voices to the chorus of night, but the soft dreamlike song of the toad was my favorite. I liked to study these little storybook creatures, and always wanted to see one "change his clothes," as Bill called it, but never did. As a toad grows, a new skin forms under his old one. After a while, as the old skin splits open up the back, the toad puts one back foot under his arm and pulls sharply, and removes that leg of his trousers. He gets out of the other leg in the same way, then puts one hand in his mouth and removes a glove, then puts the other hand in his mouth and removes the other glove. Gathering the rest of the skin in his mouth, he pulls off his shirt. Unlike the snake, which crawls away and leaves his old skin stretched on the ground, the toad *eats* his discarded garments.

All these little creatures were a part of the night, moving, feeding, hunting, calling. From back in the hills came the sharp yap-yapping of a fox. Nighthawks soared toward the moon and dropped swiftly down again uttering their tuneless cry, and there was always a killdeer who seemed to be fleeing in terror. I have no idea when the killdeer sleeps, for I have heard him all day and late into the night, even at one and two in the morning. As for the mockingbird, we were awed and silent before the wonder of his concerts in the moonlight. Following his imitative calls was like following old friends—the crow, the robin, the meadow lark, the tufted titmouse, and others—with each call repeated three times.

The darkness was full of the singing of insects and, in late summer, with the hypnotic disputes of the katydids. According to an old Indiana saying, the first katydids call just six weeks before frost. There were faint and delicate sounds, too, high in the trees, like dew or light raindrops falling upon leaves, the sound of caterpillars feeding. And there was always the call of a cricket, Indiana's watchman of the night.

Only those who grew up like James Whitcomb Riley can appreciate the full import of:

> An' little Orphant Annie says, when the blaze is
> blue,
> An' the lamp-wick sputters, an' the wind goes
> *woo-oo!*
> An' you hear the crickets quit . . .*

"*An' you hear the crickets quit* . . ."—to me, the most hair-raising line in all literature, bringing back a chilling memory of nights in the lonely country farmhouse. Shadows beyond the windows were black in the moonlight, and we

* By James Whitcomb Riley, from *Joyful Poems for Children*. Used by permission of the Bobbs-Merrill Company.

were always aware that even in our isolation, we were not free from danger. All strangers were to be regarded with suspicion, especially after sunset, for many a tramp, gypsy, and fugitive had followed our narrow country road, due to the fact that it ran parallel to the National Road farther south, and for them was much safer.

Many times I have awakened and found Virginia, my younger sister, standing beside the bed, her face and nightgown pale in the moonlight, her curly hair tumbled over her head.

"What's the matter?" I would whisper quickly.

And she would whisper back the traditional country alert, "There's somebody walking around outside!"

I would sit up and listen intently.

"I don't hear anything."

"Neither do I. *But the crickets have quit. . . .*"

Oh, blood-chilling words to any country child who, familiar since birth with the ways of nature, knows that crickets do not cease their chirring unless a footfall comes near, an intruder slips past in the darkness! Yet despite the sense of peril which such stillness may engender, the intruder may be no more than a hungry little coon bound for the orchard.

Night in the woods, especially under a full moon, has the dreamy, silvery quality of a fairy tale where everything has been touched by a summer magic. Birds, awakened by the brilliant moonlight, often trill songs, believing it is dawn. Flying squirrels, like fat little elves with enormous dark eyes, glide from one silvered tree to the other, and if the night is very still, it may be possible to hear wood mice singing. This sound, also supersonic and seldom within the range of our hearing, is said to be like the song of a canary, only very high and delicate. I always wanted to hear it but never did, though Bill claimed to have heard it twice, both times on moonlit nights.

But I have seen the wonderful and incredible sight of rabbits dancing in the moonlight, though this is not especially unusual. I know many people who have seen it, and Marjorie is one of them. As though intoxicated by the loveliness of the night, the little animals perform a graceful ballet, whirling, leaping, sailing, vaulting. The *pas de deux* of one furry little Nijinsky will linger in my memory forever.

Bill said he had watched chipmunks feeding under the moon, though most of his cronies thought he was mistaken. But Lee and I had had an excellent opportunity to be aware of a chipmunk's nocturnal activities. One of these little creatures had a hole at the base of the mulberry tree in our back yard, evidently well stocked with corn from the ears we placed near the feeder. We never saw him, however, until one spring when there was a heavy flood in our part of the country and, apparently, he was washed from his home. He promptly moved into the little green shelter house in the tree, taking all his worldy goods, about a thousand grains of corn, I should think. At night we heard him eating, eating, could glimpse him moving about. When the flood subsided, he disappeared, probably moving everything back into his hole.

It is generally believed that squirrels sleep in their nests or dens all night, but our experience with them makes us wonder whether this is really accurate. Both Mimi and Groany got up and ate in the night, and wandered about when they were not caged. Mimi would get up as often as four times during the night, sometimes to eat, sometimes to play. Lee always left her "breakfast" (one grape) in an ashtray on the bedside table, and she might get up and nibble it at two or three in the morning. More than once I have wakened to see her in the moonlight, playing with a piece of cleansing tissue, tearing it up just for fun, perhaps skipping around. Groany, too, got up and down, went in and out of his cage at night. The only time they remained in their bowls throughout the night, quietly sleeping, was when the weather was cold, rainy, foggy, or snowy.

Both our squirrels had great manual dexterity and used their hands like little monkeys, opening boxes, jars, and cans. We kept their nut meats in a small tea canister until we found them opening it and stuffing themselves between meals. Mimi would hold this little canister in the bend of her left arm, bracing it against the kitchen counter top, and with the fingers of her right hand, cleverly pry the lid from it.

They peered into cigarette boxes, looked into candy jars, opened cupboard doors (catching the bottom edges in their teeth), and we were only too thankful that they never learned to open drawers. They appear to possess the same sort of manual dexterity and intelligence as raccoons, which, in psychological tests, have shown themselves capable of escaping from complicated mazes, could promptly unfasten hooks and latches, slide bolts, and open containers.

Mimi and Groany were wild to get on my desk and meddle with all the fascinating "playthings" there—pencils, erasers, small rulers, fountain pens, rolls of cellophane tape, letter openers, and stamp boxes. They were always investigating my typewriter when my back was turned, and once when I started to use it and heard a horrible noise from inside, I opened the top and found a whole English walnut neatly deposited on the curved framework underneath.

Mimi soon discovered that there were cracked sunflower seeds (set aside for her) in a small and plump cookie jar. She would remove the lid, squat down beside the jar, brace her elbows on the rim of it, and flip the seeds into her mouth with both little hands. I tried many times to photograph this cute and unbelievable pose, but she ran away screaming angrily when I brought the camera.

During warm spring or summer days Mimi sometimes woke early from her afternoon nap and played for a while in an open but screened window. The screens were fastened with little hooks and we did not dream that she could unfasten them.

One afternoon Jamie was writing busily upstairs when a small, tawny squirrel suddenly appeared at the window beside her, took a comfortable position on the sill, and began washing its face. Many of the wild squirrels came to our windows, so she was not exactly surprised, but it occurred to her that she had never seen one with such vivid and beautiful coloring —except Mimi. Just then the visitor finished its careless ablutions and scampered off down the side of the house.

A horrible suspicion came over Jamie. She leaped up and ran downstairs and into the den where Mimi had been playing. The window screen was open, swinging in the breeze, and Mimi was gone!

Lee and I were at a supermarket, and Jamie was horrified to find herself alone with this emergency, especially since she knew Lee would be brokenhearted if anything happened to his little pet.

She rushed outside and called frantically to Mimi, who by this time had fled around to the other side of the house on the brick wall. She was now high above the street, clinging to the bricks, close to the second floor. Except for being carried in a basket from a treetop to our house, and in a car to the animal hospital, she had never been out-of-doors in all her life, and now found the experience horrifying.

The roar of the traffic beneath her, the strange world around her filled her with utter panic and she was frozen to the bricks, oblivious to everything except her own terror, paying no heed to Jamie's desperate calls. People saw what was happening and stopped to watch, and Jamie implored them, "Please go on, *please!* She'll never come to me if there are strangers around!"

Considerately enough they passed on, but Mimi would not come down. She stayed rooted to the spot, frozen with fear, but after a while her little legs began to tremble with exhaustion and her hands were losing their hold. If she fell, she would probably tumble into the street and be killed by the rushing cars.

At that moment Lee and I came home. Jamie pointed upward, and we saw Mimi clinging to the bricks with her last strength.

Wasting neither time nor words, Lee shot up the stairs and opened the window nearest (but not very near) the spot where she hung. Carefully, soothingly, he called her name, tried to coax her closer. The sound of his voice seemed to penetrate her terror and slowly, carefully, inch by inch she crept along the side of the house toward his reaching hand. Meanwhile, Lee leaned so far out of the window that I expected him to fall on his head in the street below. However, he was able to seize Mimi across the shoulders. She uttered a cry of surprise and lashed out in fright, but he kept a firm hold on her and at last drew her in through the window.

After that we reinforced all the latches and decided that we could no longer allow our pets to play around the house like kittens when we were absent. They were past the age of squirrel childhood, would get into more and more mischief, and must have cages in which to stay when we were unable to watch them, not just for sleeping, as was Groany's small cage.

With their many needs in mind, Jamie and Lee designed and built two cages just alike. They were about the size and shape of telephone booths, but a little less than five feet tall. Each had, near the top, a door that opened downward.

Just inside this door was a fairly broad feeding-and-sleeping shelf sixteen inches from the top. It was seven inches wide at the narrow end, jutted to eleven inches wide at the other end, where stood a sleeping bowl firmly anchored and fully equipped with small terry blankets.

At the back of the cage, two and a half inches from the back wall, was a "resting shelf" (two and a half inches wide), which reached all the way across. Such a ledge is a favorite retreat of all fox squirrels, and they usually lie there with head and body stretched out, arms and legs dangling, utterly relaxed. At other times they will lie with hind legs stretched back (as dogs do), and their heads laid down on little fists.

The cage walls were formed from a single length of welded wire fabric (one-inch by two-inch mesh) stood on edge, and the cage itself was twenty-two inches wide and twenty-four inches deep. The open side was closed by bending in small lengths of the wire left for this purpose, and the top (cut in one piece) was attached in the same way.

The door (ten inches high, ten and a half inches wide) was cut out in the center of the cage front, just above the feeding shelf. The lower edge of this door was attached to the edge of the feeding shelf with "hinges" that were really small staples.

In the bottom of each cage was an old refrigerator tray which filled it (resting on a plywood base) and which slid in and out through a space left for it. It was kept lined with newspapers.

Each cage contained a small "tree" installed before the walls were closed, a sturdy branch cut from an apple tree, stood upright, and fastened to the walls with brads. The squirrels played here, ran up and down, and nibbled the bark.

When we fed them in their cages, we opened the door and set the little plate of food inside. We then closed the door and secured it with a twist of wire. However, we did not fully appreciate even yet the manual dexterity of our pets. They promptly untwisted these wires with their clever little fingers, tossed the door down, and came out. We tested them by twisting the wire (thin picture wire) many times in complicated ways, and though it took them longer to solve the problem, they always unfastened the wires and emerged sooner than we expected. We then used snap clothespins, which they promptly unsnapped with their teeth and threw on the floor. It seemed likely that they would be able to open latches, too, so we fastened the doors with metal snaps, such as are used on the leashes of small dogs, and these they could not open.

The cages were handsome, comfortable, and secure, but when we put Mimi and Groany inside for the first time, they ran up and down, squalled with rage, banged and clanged, and would not be quiet, would not climb their trees, lie on their resting shelves, or even look at their food. The din they made was absolutely deafening, and went on for three or four hours. At last we gave up and opened the doors. They immediately changed cages, and were content from that day on, for reasons which will never be known.

Marjorie and Carl had often observed the woodland custom which they called "home swapping" and thought it might be due to the discomfort of poorly planned shelters. They were careful, therefore, to provide for their little wild creatures homes of the types, materials, and dimensions recommended by naturalists and other authorities. And the little creatures promptly moved in, just as the books said they would, but after a little while, they were not there any more. During a single day in the woods Marjorie found flying squirrels in the bluebird house, an owl in the squirrel house, a squirrel in the wood-duck house, and a possum in the doghouse.

Our small green house with the natural knothole for an entrance had been used as a temporary shelter, resting place, feeding station, and sleeping room by the chipmunk, and by many wild squirrels. In time it became the favorite retreat of a female fox squirrel so tiny and young that we called her "the Little Girl."

There are some squirrels that seem to prefer the company of human beings, and she was one of them. Like Sharley, she followed at our heels, "called" us to the window when she was hungry, and "talked" to us happily when we appeared. More than once she tried to go into the house with us, but we felt sure that she would have been panic-stricken, once inside, and anyway we did not want a wild squirrel (which sometimes carries mites, fleas, and infections) to get close to our pampered pets.

One afternoon, when I glanced out at the small green house and saw a figure in it, I assumed that it was the Little Girl, who often took a siesta there. It occurred to me, however, that her fur seemed unusually light and rough, and a closer look showed me that the occupant was *not* a young squirrel, but a young possum!

I have always had an aversion toward animals with long pointed noses and sharp pointed teeth, such as foxes, wolves, weasels, and possums—an aversion rooted, I have no doubt, in my childhood terror of "The Wolf" pictured in *Grimm's Fairy Tales.* So I was never much interested in possums, despite their place in Indiana wildlife—though this one was small and clean and rather cute. I could see his long gray face, the pink tip of his nose, and his shiny black eyes.

Through the binoculars, I studied him more carefully. It was late afternoon, and I believe he was just waking up. Lazily, he turned on his back, sat (like Groany) on his tail bone, and began to wash his bright pink hands and feet, licking them like a kitten. I could see that even his teeth, showing through his "perpetual grin," were bright pink. I wondered if he had been lured to this location by the presence of our heavily-laden grapevine, for there were grape leaves protruding from his doorway. Evidently he had snapped them off and carried them to bed with him.

I have never seen a possum making a nest, but can't imagine anything that would be more fascinating to watch. His residence is often quite temporary, as he has a habit of taking up his abode in the homes of other animals, who frequently evict him when they return. Placidly enough he moves on, and may sleep in a different place nearly every night.

For his own comfort, however, he lines his sleeping room with nesting material, especially leaves. He gathers into his mouth as many leaves as possible, passes them back under his body to be grasped by his tail. The process is continued until he has a large bundle to carry away in this thin circle, after which he takes these, and perhaps still another mouthful, into whatever residence he has chosen, and makes a cosy bed.

Later in the afternoon Lee came home, cut the grass, and weeded some flowers, while the possum watched him with the interest and curiosity of all wild things. When he walked over to the birdbath, just under the tree where the house was located, the possum saw him coming and quickly turned over, presenting the black part of his fur to the knothole entrance. It was as though he had declared, "There's nobody, but nobody, in this empty black hole!" And it certainly *looked* empty.

Apparently he was waiting for darkness, since possums are nocturnal animals. About 7 P.M., near dusk, I saw him slip down the tree and lose himself in the heavy growth of ivy and violet leaves which we had planted there as a cover for our wild friends. He may have dined on the nearly ripe grapes, since possums are fond of fruit, and also on the snacks we provided for him. Near the back gate, in the shelter of the cover growth, Lee left an apple, half an ear of green corn, and a bone to gnaw. Later, through the darkness, we heard an enthusiastic *crunch-crunch*, and when we inspected the picnic area around midnight, both the possum *and* the snacks were gone.

"I think he means to stay," said Lee, and added, "I'm afraid our poor Little Girl has lost her favorite shelter."

Toward morning we heard a terrific commotion near the back of the house, in the vicinity of the tree, but it was of short duration, and when we peered out into the dawn's early light, there was nothing to be seen. At breakfast time, however, we observed that the small house was fully occupied, and *not* by the possum. There, surrounded by somewhat wilted grape leaves, sat the Little Girl, calmly and firmly awaiting her usual breakfast.

X

Children of the back country are taught from their earliest years to beware of unfamiliar plants and berries because so many are harmful. Indeed, in the woodlands of Indiana poison hangs over our heads, springs up at our feet, nudges our elbows. Poison threatens us in tender roots, lush and lovely leaves, beautiful flowers, and mellow fruits. It spreads along our country roads and creeks, across our summer meadowlands, over our forest floors, our swamps and hilltops.

Plant poisoning is an old and familiar subject which has been accurately described by Hippocrates and other scholars of the ancient world. All of us remember learning in school that Socrates went to his death by drinking "hemlock," but the nature of this poison was unknown to us. We were inclined to think of it as an obscure brew belonging to an obscure age, and had no notion that it could be found almost under our feet.

Children on picnics and other outings have more than once tasted and eaten the water hemlock, which attracts people and animals because it has the appearance of a fresh and tasty salad green; it has leaves like parsley, roots similar to parsnips, and seeds resembling caraway. A few hours after eating a little of this plant, children and animals alike have died in dreadful convulsions. There are records, too, of deaths resulting not from eating, but only from chewing the deadly pungent roots, and even from drinking water out of the pools in which they grew. Children have been poisoned by blowing whistles made from the hollow stems.

White snakeroot is, of course, one of the deadliest of plants, causes the deaths of many animals, and may be spread to humans through the milk of cows which have eaten it.

Among the common Indiana wild flowers which are poisonous (wholly, or in part) are such dainty blossoms as Dutchman's breeches, buttercups, dwarf larkspur, black-eyed Susan, blue flags, bloodroot, May apple, and lobelia (Indian tobacco). Butter-and-eggs, the pretty yellow-and-white flower seen in gardens and around the countryside, is a virulent poison. Early settlers steeped it in milk and used it to kill flies.

Other very poisonous plants are the oleander (used in some parts of the world in rat poison), narcissus, iris, star-of-Bethlehem, lily of the valley, snow-on-the-mountain, larkspur, foxglove, aconite, and English ivy.

Castor beans are very attractive to children as "play food" and they are likely to eat them, as it does not occur to a child to think of beans as dangerous. Yet they contain one of the world's most virulent poisons, comparable to rattlesnake venom, and a single bean can be a lethal dose. Considering how strictly poison must be labeled when prepared for household use, it is surprising that seed companies have never been required to label poisonous garden flowers for the protection of children and to inform their mothers, all of whom cannot be botanists.

Dangerous wild fruits include the unripe and uncooked berries of the deadly nightshade, holly berries, baneberries, the berries of mistletoe and bittersweet, the Jerusalem cherry, uncooked pokeberries and their roots, unripe ground cherries, the bright red berries of the daphne, and the "berries" of the burning bush, also known as wahoo. The fruit of the May apple is harmless if *really* ripe, but since this is an extremely poisonous plant, it seems prudent to avoid it altogether.

The black cherry tree is deadly—bark, seeds, sprouts and leaves. The seeds and bark of the black locust (*not* the honey locust) are so poisonous that animals have died from drinking water in which they had soaked. Oak leaves are extremely dangerous, as are the leaves of the wild cherry tree, especially if they are wilted. Buckeye sprouts and seeds can be fatal, and many children have lost their lives by eating the shiny mahogany-hued "nuts" of this tree. (True, Indian women knew how to cook them in a way that destroyed their poisonous properties, but such experiments are not for us.) The leaves of the common peach tree contain one of the most virulent poisons known, as do ordinary rhubarb leaves.

Jimson Weed is famous for its lethal properties. (Legend says the name is a corruption of "Jamestown," where hungry pioneers cooked and ate this plant, and died from the effects.)

Both children and adults have been poisoned by eating (or only tasting) a back-country plant which resembles wild onion or garlic, but is really the death camas.

Even the common Irish potato can be dangerous at times. There is a poisonous material called solanin in the "eyes" and sprouts, especially if they have been in the sun. When turned green by sunlight, the potatoes can be very harmful and some people have died from eating them.

One of the bewildering things about nature is that a harmless plant may bear poisonous berries, a wholly uninjurious flower may have deadly leaves, edible fruits may come from a tree with poisonous bark, or from a plant with poisonous roots. Some plants are dangerous when raw but not when cooked, when green but not when ripe. Some are poisonous at one time of the year, but not at another. Some lose their poisonous properties when dried, some do not. Some are rendered harmless by sunlight, some are rendered harmful.

Thus people who know the woods teach their children *never*

to taste nut, berry, seed, grass, fruit, plant, flower, pod, root, or bark until they have learned to really *know* the difference between the many noxious plants and the many harmless and delicious ones.

We never gave our little pets food from the wilds without first checking to be certain that it was uninjurious. They seemed to crave mulberry leaves, but even these had to be fed sparingly and with caution, for they affect squirrels as catnip affects kittens, and can be overstimulating. Actually, their favorite greenery was lettuce, and we were often thankful that their appetites were less demanding and eccentric than that of the caterpillar.

Their lives seemed to governed by a self-imposed routine that rarely varied. Each morning, Mimi rose and ate her one grape, then hopped to the window sill and gazed out the window for exactly five minutes. She then hopped back into bed and nuzzled Lee to awaken him. Patiently she waited (in a squirrel's usual "waiting pose") while he dressed. Then she leaped upon his shoulder and rode to the kitchen with one little hand clutching his collar. This was the only time she ever held to his collar, but it was an unfailing part of her morning ritual.

At first, when Lee rose to dress, she would leap upon his bare back, ready to travel, a leap that resulted in giving him some sharp scratches. Very quickly, however, he taught her to wait until he had put on his shirt. She would watch him eagerly and sharply, sometimes with the little bounces that showed she was ready to jump, and the *moment* his shirt was on his shoulder, so was she! One morning, just as he was getting ready to don his trousers, she ran up the legs. Nothing was ever funnier than her really baffled expression when she reached the waist and found nobody in them.

Groany was sweet, loving, and obedient, but Mimi was as naughty as a wayward child, and would sometimes get up at 5 A.M. in order to get into mischief while we were asleep. She would slip out of bed and play in forbidden places, doing forbidden things. Then, when tired, she would slip back into bed, take a nap, and wake up again, ready for her morning routine, as though she had been there all the time.

Usually I woke up, too, and unknown to her, watched to see what she would do. She went upstairs and pilfered Jamie's desk, then dashed back carrying in her mouth an eraser or a paper clip to be hidden hastily in her bowl. She explored my typewriter, tried to chew my pencils, opened cans of nuts or seeds in the kitchen and helped herself.

Both squirrels soon learned that goodies were often found under lids. However, they would lift a lid that was lying flat on a table or counter top and look under it just as hopefully as they looked into a container. They seemed to have no sense of proportion, and when Mimi was hunting for Lee, she might peer into a cigarette box, a tea canister, or a bedroom slipper. For a long time, they seemed unable to realize that our feet belonged to us, and Groany often attacked Jamie's white Indian moccasins when they approached him, evidently thinking them a team of enemies. When she wore dark shoes, he did not seem to mind, or perhaps to notice. The white ones were his foes and every time he saw them he would, if possible, charge them and rip off a few beads.

On pleasant summer mornings our squirrels played in the open screened windows, skipping, bouncing, and cavorting on the sills. Sometimes the wild squirrels would come and try to make friends with them, but they were either ignored or haughtily rejected. Once a little male climbed up on the screen and challenged Groany with an insolent "*Tut-tut-tut-tut-tut!*" which caused Groany to fly into an absolute rage and lunge at him savagely.

One of the strangest sounds they made was done with their teeth, an incredibly rapid clicking which when loud, plainly expressed anger and when soft, seemed to indicate contentment or pleasure. Groany seldom screamed, but Mimi often did, especially when strangers wanted to look at her.

They learned to know what we meant when we said, "*No, no!*" "*Too hard!*" and "*Come here!*" When Jamie announced, "*Here comes Lee!*" Mimi would immediately jump up in her bowl and start looking for him. When Groany got into mischief, I would tell him, "*I'm ashamed!*" and he would stop whatever he was doing, reproved by the tone of my voice.

We learned to interpret the sounds they made, such as the low grunting "*Mm . . . mm . . . mm*" which expressed love and pleasure. When they were ill, this sound became a pitiful prolonged "*Mmmmmmmmmmmm . . . mmmmmmmmmmm.*" When they wanted something, it was a begging "*Mmmmm . . . mmmm . . . mmmm,*" and in another tone, this could be interpreted as a demand.

Of course, their signal of acute distress was the shrill "bird call" we had heard from Shad, like the one Marjorie heard from her little waif Patsy. When angry, Groany might utter a sharp, warning "*Chik!*" Mimi said "*Chek!*" instead. A tiny squealing cry indicated helpless fear, the sound made by Mimi when the veterinarian gave her a shot for pneumonia, and when he clipped her teeth.

During Groany's brief adolescence, he became absolutely unbearable for his constant complaints. Nothing pleased him, and he responded to everything with a groaning sound that was something like "*Wraaaa . . . wraaaa . . . wraaaa,*" the sound responsible for his nickname. As he matured, however, he ceased this sound and never repeated it, but during his "teens" you had only to touch him with one finger and he would begin to lament as though he were the most abused creature in the world.

When she was older, Mimi would pursue Groany with the call of female coquetry often heard in the woods in the summer, "*Waa . . . waa . . . waaa,*" and then run and hide. When they romped and played up and down adjacent sides of their cages, or lay facing each other upon their resting shelves, their mouths kept moving as though they were communicating, but we could hear nothing.

On several occasions, though, I have heard them utter a strange sound almost like a high thin scream, so small and faint that it was easy to think I had imagined it. I heard this from Groany when he demanded that I stop work and play with him. I heard it from Mimi when she was thirsty and wanted a drink *at once*. Neither Lee nor Jamie ever heard it at all, and I can only believe it was one of the "supersonic" sounds which seldom falls in our auditory range. (I have been blessed, however, with very keen ears.)

Groany would often slip away from me and run upstairs to explore. This was forbidden territory, though, and as soon as I discovered his absence, I would go up and find him and "herd" him down the steps in front of me. All the way down, he grumbled and groused like a grumpy little old man, "*Rrr-rrrrr-rrrrrrrr-rrrrrrr. . . .*" Later he learned to trick me. He would proceed down the steps meekly enough and then, just before he reached the bottom, suddenly whirl and streak back up again, passing me like a meteor.

After that, I gave him no opportunity for tricks, but simply snatched him up and carried him down, which so outraged him that he struggled furiously, uttering the squirrel's expression of angry protest which I can only describe as a loud "*Tcheng! . . . tcheng! . . . tcheng!*" In time he learned that when I found him, there was no reprieve. Resignedly, he would climb to my shoulder and ride downstairs without protest.

The squirrels had many interesting postures related to certain emotions and responses:

Waiting: When waiting (as Mimi waited for Lee to carry her to the kitchen), they sat up very straight and tall, eyes straight ahead, hands clasped on stomach.

Listening: When listening intently (and sometimes when

anxious or just curious), they leaned forward, one hand lifted to the breast, one of their cutest poses.

Merriment: When having fun, they might "grin" as a dog "grins."

Anger: They chattered or barked, sitting up straight, jerking tail round and round in fury.

Fear: They ran with tail lowered, took refuge in a hiding place or behind us, clinging to our backs.

Hurt Feelings: They crouched in a corner, hanging head.

Intense Pain: They cried out, running blindly.

Sleepy: They stretched full length, while standing, much as a tiger stretches, mouth open to amazing width, claws extended and gripping shelf or other surface. The yawning pose.

Sulking: They turned backs, ignored all attentions.

Guilt: Both Mimi and Groany exhibited guilt feelings when caught doing things they had been trained not to do, such as stealing sugar. Mimi would lap sugar from the bowl as fast as possible, all the while looking from one side to the other to see if we were coming.

Jealousy: Though less apparent than jealousy between domestic pets such as dogs, it did exist. When Lee petted Groany and made a fuss over him, Mimi's face took on a woebegone expression, and she drew herself up into a tight little knot of misery as she watched.

To say that a squirrel is capable of shame or embarrassment sounds more than a little far-fetched, yet I did see something of this sort from Groany once.

We had a paper boy who was fascinated by the squirrels (he called them Grundy and Mamie) and was always coming in to see them. For some reason, both of them feared him and would turn their backs to him or hide in their bowls.

One day, when he was standing by the cage, I reached inside to give Groany an almond. Groany mistook my hand for that of the paper boy, charged me, and started to bite me. When he saw it was *me*, he dropped the hand, scurried into a corner of his cage, and sat there with his head low, the very picture of abject humiliation.

Once we saw Groany assume a posture so astonishing that even while we looked at him, we could not believe our eyes. He was sitting in his bowl, had his elbow propped upon the rim, and was leaning his head against his hand. When resting, both squirrels could look extremely solemn and meditative, as though pondering all the ills and burdens of humanity.

They barked at sounds they disliked or did not recognize, such as the call of a bluejay and the humming of my blender. Barking, I think, indicates protest or surprise, and is most often heard when the squirrel is startled by an unfamiliar sight or sound. Chattering was a means of attracting attention and expressing irritation, possibly of giving a warning, too.

When they first lived with us, many of the household sounds frightened them, but after a while they became accustomed to blender, garbage disposal, the closing of the refrigerator door, the perking of coffee, the whirr of the electric mixer, and did not even open an eye. However, they never ceased to be afraid of the vacuum cleaner, and always hid when they heard it. Mimi feared it most and would dive into her bowl or huddle under the covers on Lee's bed whenever this dust-breathing monster approached.

If they wanted to attract our attention and perhaps be taken out to play, they would run up and down their cages, jump from side to side, chew the metal or knock on it. Groany, by way of calling us, learned to make a very penetrating and annoying sound by catching a wire of the mesh in his teeth and twanging it like a harp.

When Groany was a baby, almost anyone would have had him put to death and considered it an act of mercy, but I had saved him and he rewarded me with unceasing love. He preferred me to anyone else, even to Mimi, and followed at my heels like a puppy. He would leap to my shoulder, nuzzle my face affectionately, greet me by hugging my forearm with both his furry little arms, or hugging one of my ankles in the same way. Lee would sometimes open his cage in the mornings and let him come into the bedroom to find me. Many times I have been awakened by a furry little body jumping lightly upon my midriff, and a warm little tongue licking my ear. Often, when I passed his cage, he would reach out one hand and touch my shoulder, begging me to stop and play.

One day when I was lying on the sofa reading, I felt a bony little hand clutch my forefinger and there was Groany, curled up beside me, holding on gently while I read. After that, he often held my finger while I read or studied, and sometimes he would lie flat on his tummy, facing me, holding my first two fingers with his little hands, resting his chin on the space between them.

Mimi loved napping in a real bed at all times, was never afraid there, and even in warm weather wanted lots and lots of cover. Groany, too, liked to get into a real bed, but was afraid to be under the covers alone. This "big dark place" seemed to terrify him, but if he could hold on to me, he did not mind. So, holding on to my hand, he cuddled down under the cover and slept contentedly while I read in bed.

On hot summer days they were sometimes uncomfortable in their fur coats. I cooled them by gently stroking them with a damp cloth, which frightened them at first, but pleased them later. We gave them ice cubes to lick, which they found delightful, and Mimi licked a hole in hers. Groany, who was very resourceful, sometimes lay down on his. Both were spoiled about iced food and drink. Mimi scorned watermelon that was not iced, and Groany would drink from the tap only when the water was *very* cold. He drank occasionally in summer, but Mimi did not, though she sometimes accepted a little watermelon juice *if* it was iced.

They slept through the hottest part of the day, sometimes curled up in their bowls, but often stretched out on their resting shelves. On hot summer nights I often let Groany sleep on a kitchen window sill. Squirrels will not sleep (except for naps) without making some sort of bed, and I usually left a few freshly washed "blankets" for him. But one night I forgot, and when I got up next morning, there was Groany asleep on the kitchen sill lying on a neatly arranged dish towel, his head on a pot holder.

Many squirrels are very clean little animals and even in the woods throw their bedding out to be "sunned and aired," then carry it back inside and rearrange it. Groany, being very immaculate, was always tossing his blankets out of his bowl, and onto the floor of his cage, where we replaced them with fresh ones. Mimi, however, tossed out only her top ones, not wishing to disturb the many treasures and tidbits she had secretly buried underneath. We had to wait until she was out of the room in order to recover the numerous items she had patted away between separate folds of terry cloth—Lee's nail clippers, one of my earrings, and a few old apple peels, for instance. We rarely saw Groany take anything, but found amazing objects in his bowl, including a full-size saucer, a heavy ashtray, and a darning egg, all of which he had obviously carried "home" in his mouth when we weren't looking.

One year we had a heat wave so sweltering that even Mimi had to seek coolness. One night, as though wretchedly hot, she emerged from under the covers at Lee's feet and started looking around for material to make a cooler sleeping place. Lee and I had been sitting up in bed reading, and we watched with great interest while she worked.

Glancing around, she saw the clothing Lee had laid out for morning. One by one, she took his socks in her mouth, carried them to the sill of the open window nearest the bed, and laid them flat, patting them out smoothly with her little hands, the cute gesture so characteristic of all squirrels. She then went back, picked up his T-shirt, and dragged it to the sill. After that, she brought his shorts. All these were made into a neat bed, with much arranging, pulling, folding, and an enormous amount of patting. At last it suited her, but she had no wish to sleep there alone, she wanted Lee to come with her.

As eagerly as a puppy, she ran to him and looked up into his face, then ran to the window sill and rearranged her bed, then back to him again, and back to the sill. As plainly as though in words, she kept saying, "Just come and see how nice it is, how soft and cool!" Lee was enchanted, and thought her the smartest and most lovable little animal to exist since the world began.

One thing I had always observed about the squirrels was that they showed certain indications of being left-handed. Mimi held to Lee's collar with her left hand when she rode out to breakfast, struck at me with her left hand when she lost her temper, reached for "lollipops" and other treats with her left hand more often than with her right. Groany always held on to my finger with his left hand, and when "listening" lifted his left hand to his breast. In this pose Mimi, too, lifted her left hand. In most of their activities, however, they used both hands at once, and usually reached out to take things in their mouths, not in their hands.

Though both Mimi and Groany appeared to be very healthy after they were grown, there were times when we had to resort to "home remedies" in order to help them. The veterinarians kept telling us that they were very sensitive little creatures, and could not be given an anesthetic without extreme risk. Also that medicine must never be forced down them (except in a life-and-death situation, with no alternative left), as they might die of shock.

Once when Groany seemed to have a stomach upset, I gave him half a Tums. He sat up and ate it and promptly got well. We regulated their bowels when they were babies by increasing or decreasing the amount of syrup in their formulas, as is done for children. Later, we found that butternut squash has useful laxative properties for adult squirrels.

Also as a laxative, mineral oil (ten drops) was suggested by the veterinarian. I put this on Groany's watermelon seeds or on his sliced cucumbers, which were slick anyway. If the oil was not absolutely fresh, though, he would promptly detect this and refuse it. Later I found that corn oil was just as effective and more palatable, in his estimation. I put it in a plastic medicine dropper, slipped the end into one corner of his mouth, and squeezed very gently, giving him just *a little* at a time. He drank as though he liked it, and we had no trouble at all.

We soon found that the squirrels were natural-born pilferers and would steal from us, and from each other, with great speed, skill, and dexterity. Whenever we suddenly missed anything, we would say, "Look in Mimi's bowl!" In Mimi's bowl we found, besides many other things, Lee's watch, Jamie's bracelet, my nail polish. I caught Mimi running away with one of my lipsticks, and later with a small vial of perfume. (They always took great interest in anything shaped like a stick.) A great jingling attracted my attention one day, just in time for me to see Groany scampering toward his cage with Lee's car keys in his mouth, hurrying to bury this wonderful find in his bowl. He also buried a nutcracker there. Once, when I was trying to make some notes, Groany snatched my pen and fled with it, and while I was running after him, Mimi took off with my reading glasses. Certain woods animals and a number of birds will steal bright or unusual objects, carry them home, and hide them, especially crows and bluejays.

Once Marjorie went with us to southern Indiana, to the farm home of Lloyd and Adele Beesley, who have spent their lives in these wild and picturesque hills, and know them intimately. That afternoon, Adele took us to a dense and rugged woods to see a showy orchis she had found, and while we were there Marjorie absently laid down her prescription sunglasses. Later she forgot all about them, and went home without them. A day or so afterward she remembered where she had last worn them, and thought it would be easy to find them again.

"I know just *exactly* where I left them," she kept saying.

Adele told her she didn't think they'd be there *now*, but she'd look for them anyway, just to be sure. And she did, but they were gone.

"Buried away in a nest somewhere," she surmised.

Lloyd laughed and added, "Most likely some little squirrel is looking through them now!"

Squirrel nests, blown down or abandoned, often yield some fascinating "treasures." Once, in a nest blown down near the park, Lee found a tennis ball, and laughed to think of this little animal streaking home with the biggest "nut" in the world.

Whenever Groany snatched up anything he wasn't supposed to have, he would fight for it with indignant squalls, defy Lee or Jamie if they came near him, even charge them and try to bite them. However, I could take it from him without fear of reprisal. He might be furious, squall and scream and kick at me, but he *never* charged me or tried to bite me, no matter how angry he became.

Squirrels are always getting into hassels over food, and Mimi still filched morsels from Groany, perhaps even a delicacy he was engaged in eating at the moment. In a terrible rage, he would fly after her, and they would go round and round, both squalling and screaming. But he was faster than she, and when she saw that he was about to overtake her, she would leap upon Lee for protection or, when desperate, upon Jamie or me. From this safe haven she would chatter at him with maddening, jeering insolence.

After we had cages for them, Groany would slip into Mimi's cage and eat the very same kind of food he had refused to eat in his own cage. She would do the same. Sometimes he would catch her, or she would catch him. Then there were screams of rage and a furious chase, which the insulted one quickly abandoned in order to return to his ravaged quarters and inspect the extent of the damage.

I believe this pilfering accounts for some of the furious quarrels I have seen in the woods—one squirrel caught another stealing from him. I remember one violent battle which broke out between two squirrels high up in a tree, in a woods where I had been hunting. I stood watching them, astonished by their rage, until one suddenly knocked the other out of the tree. He came down through the branches with a crashing sound, struck the earth with a thud, and I thought of course he was killed. But he ran as soon as he hit the ground, dashed up a neighboring tree, and did not seem at all injured or even shaken.

In their own woods Marjorie and Carl tried to provide suitable homes for the wild creatures, and knowing that squirrel-pilfering sometimes extends to taking cosy spots away from birds, they sent for a government bulletin showing how to build a squirrel-proof house for their wood ducks.

This dwelling, long and tubular and made of metal, was lined with chicken wire and had a hole near the top. It was suspended from a branch near the pond and the wood ducks moved into it for a time, but later moved out again.

One very hot summer afternoon Marjorie called, asking for aid. She had looked out into the woods and had seen a young squirrel hanging from the house by one foot, evidently caught in the chicken wire that protruded from it. The squirrel had been struggling violently for some time, and she feared it would be injured or die of shock.

Lee happened to be at home, so we drove in haste to her house, taking a long ladder which he set up against the tree. Seeing him approach, the squirrel (a pretty little female) became frantic with fear, fought desperately to loosen her foot, and was finally able to break free. With a terrific leap, she sprang into another tree and streaked away.

(Mimi had broken one of her toes, when she was a baby,

by catching it in a window latch in the very same way. She fought so violently in her panic that she injured herself before we could quiet her or release the latch.)

"That house is a hazard, anyway," Marjorie stated. "I've seen other animals caught in it, and now that the wood ducks have left, it serves no purpose. So let's take it down."

Lee agreed, and while we held the ladder, he went up, slipped the squirrel-proof house off the branch, and slowly lowered it to the ground. When he came down, he removed the top and to our astonishment we found inside, not an abandoned wood-duck nest, but a fairly new squirrel nest.

In the middle of the leaves huddled two tiny babies, obviously just born, both as pink as strawberry ice cream and as naked as a light bulb! Behold, the government's squirrel-proof house held a whole family!

In dismay we hastily replaced the top and restored the house to the tree. Then we removed the ladder and went inside, watching from the kitchen window to see if the little mother returned. There is a persistent belief that a mother will abandon young which humans have touched, though we have never found this to be true. Nevertheless, Lee rubbed the house and his hands with fresh mint leaves to remove the human smell and allay some of her fears.

Time passed. After a while we saw her come back, moving very cautiously, and slip into the nest. Evidently she had come to see whether the babies were still alive and unharmed. Reassured, she soon emerged and went away again.

More time went by. The afternoon was fading, the sky was growing dark, and a summer storm was brewing. Some drops fell from the heavy clouds, and thunder muttered in the distance. Then we saw the mother again. More boldly this time, she hastened to the tree, ran up, and slipped into the nest. In a flash she was out again, but this time she moved very slowly and carefully. Taking turns at the binoculars, we watched her and saw that she carried one of the babies in her mouth, holding it gently by the skin of its stomach. Meanwhile, the baby clung to her fur with its little hands and kept its tail around her neck. Handling the tiny burden with care, she slipped off into the woods. Somewhere she had found another den, had quickly made another nest perhaps.

Her journey was not long. Soon we saw her streaking back to the tree. Again she went in and again came out slowly and cautiously, carrying the second and last baby in her mouth. By the time the storm broke, she and her babies were settled in their new home, out of the rain, and safely away from the intrusive kindness of blundering humans.

About fifteen minutes after her last trip, and just before the rain began, a young male squirrel appeared, went up the tree, looked into the house several times, as though hunting for something, and at last went away. We thought this might be the father of the babies. I told Marjorie about the theories of Bill and some of the other old hunters—that while the mother gave birth and tended her babies, the father lived nearby; that when the babies were old enough to live alone, the mother left them, returned to her mate, and started a new family. Of course, she might be deprived of her first mate early in life if, like Sharley's mate, he happened to be a "traveler" or if he was killed during the hunting season, when so many male squirrels are shot.

When we saw the wild squirrels playing merrily, scampering about the trees, enjoying the fresh buds and the cool fresh air, we pitied our little pets, feeling that they had been deprived of a birthright. In the beginning, Lee had talked about setting them free eventually, perhaps in Marjorie's woods, but it became more and more evident, as time passed, that they could not care for themselves. I pointed out that Groany had never learned to open a nut, and had lost the sight in one eye, that Mimi's teeth would keep growing until she starved, and anyway, after the pneumonia, she had to be carefully protected from the cold. Too, we had become so attached to them that it was heartbreaking to think of turning them out and then wondering and worrying about them. The possibility so upset me that once I dreamed I saw a red-tailed hawk swoop down on Groany's sightless side and seize him.

It was a part of Mimi's daily routine that every evening, just at sunset, she went to the den window, put one little hand against the pane, and sat there gazing out at the evening until dusk. We thought perhaps she missed, instinctively, the life she had never had, and felt very sorry for her.

Therefore we decided to let them spend some time out-of-doors. One bright summer day we took them out in the yard, cages and all, but instead of being pleased with the cool shade, the warm sun, and the fresh air, they hated them, were terrified by the feel of the wind and the sound of the leaves. Mimi screamed in protest, and Groany hid himself under the blankets in his bowl.

We tried many times to give them a bit of outdoor life, but they wanted no part of the big, wide, wonderful world—except through a screened window. And even this wasn't always satisfactory. Once, when Groany was playing on the sill, it started to rain and a few drops struck him sharply. In fear and outrage he whirled furiously, charged the rain, and tried to bite it.

When we found the squirrels, we thought how interesting and pleasant it would be if they ever grew tame enough to recognize us individually, and perhaps come when we called. Certainly we never dreamed that they would hold our hands, watch our TV, climb into bed with us, and steal our jewelry!

XI Fall is perhaps the easiest time of year for an Indiana fox squirrel. The days are warm and beautiful and the countryside sweet with grapes and apples. The sun is benevolent, and wherever squirrels look, there is an abundance of things good to eat, easy to carry, delightful to store. Cornfields are no longer green, but the dry and rustling rows are heavy with hard yellow ears dear to the appetites of furry little animals.

A squirrel may seize an ear of corn in his mouth and carry it nearly half a mile to a tree, a stump, a rail fence, or whatever festive board he has selected as his favorite and his own. Here songbirds, quail, and pheasants enjoy the crumbs from his table.

No person brought up in Indiana could be away from it in the fall without a sharp nostalgia for that incredibly beautiful season "*when the frost is on the punkin and the fodder's in the shock*," as James Whitcomb Riley knew it.* And despite modern farming methods and modern farm machinery, there are still many places in southern Indiana where one may see "the fodder in the shock"—cornstalks gathered up and tied into cone-like sheaves, each standing straight in the harvested

* From *Joyful Poems for Children*. Used by permission of the Bobbs-Merrill Company.

field. These rows and rows of corn shocks, seen through the fall mist under a tawny September moon, look exactly like tepees silent and deserted, the ghostly village of Indians long dead.

By day the woods is full of autumn glory—brilliant yellow maples, red and orange maples, flaming oaks, every tree adorned with its own gypsy colors. The sassafras sends tongues of red fire along the fence rows, the staghorn sumac lifts it own harvest horn of tiny red berries above brilliant leaves. Along the roadsides, fall flowers design a tapestry of eloquently blended hues, the purple of thistles and New England asters and ironweed, the rich red of pokeberries, butter-yellow primroses, pale-blue St. Mary asters, rose and white and pink knotweed, acres of wild sunflowers, nodding goldenrod, the pink heads of wild bergamot which the pioneers called Oswego tea.

Pasture lands are filled with the incessant hum and leap and movement of little creatures nearing the end of summer, fat black crickets, restless katydids and grasshoppers, the dazzling flash of dragonflies over smooth ponds and quiet streams, and the sailing past of butterflies, especially the orange-and-black monarchs. These creatures swarm in fall, and migrate southward, sometimes halting to rest in a woods where trees covered by their many wings burst suddenly into orange bloom in the sun.

At night it is not uncommon to hear the sound of click beetles, often called "tick bugs" in the back country. An old Indiana superstition regards this sound as a token of death because "the beetle is ticking away the life of someone dear to you, and you will hear of this death in a few days." Another superstition says that if a measuring worm (cankerworm) crawls or falls upon you, as it may in autumn, he is "measuring you for a coffin" and you are marked for death. However, since children (and some adults) are disturbed by this suggestion, it is often changed to "measuring you for new clothes."

On the grass a huge daddy longlegs makes his way, the creature with the longest legs in the world, considering the size of his body. "*If you kill him, you will have a poor harvest*"—an old English saying which may have come to Indiana with the pioneers. Children stop him, hold one of his legs under a forefinger, and demand, "Which way are the cows?" The daddy longlegs lifts another leg and appears to point, and in this direction (folklore tells us) you will find strayed or grazing cattle without hunting them, saving yourself and them a great deal of time.

Green walnuts may be found on the ground, each with a hole bitten in it by a squirrel. The little animals cut the nuts from the trees and bite them, then drop them below. Flies enter the hole and lay eggs, and when these hatch, the larvae soften the hull and make it easy to remove. Without this treatment, it would be very difficult to hull and bury the nuts before frost because, according to a back-country saying, *nothing* (except a miser) is "tighter'n the bark on a green walnut."

The wind rises, the leaves drift down, the sun shines on the fields and orchards, on the golden abundance of pumpkins and squash and corn and persimmons and pears and yellow apples, the purple harvest of grapes and plums. The days are full of the murmurous humming and singing of insects in the grass. Then one clear and starry night, the prophecy of the katydids comes true, and a heavy frost falls upon the countryside. In the morning, gardens and fields and roadsides are brown and sere, and there is no sound, no sound at all. The sudden silence is a thing of sadness, for many little creatures are dead, many have vanished, and the end of summer has come.

Yet frost is awaited with eagerness, for it brings the beechnuts tumbling from the trees, ripens the wild grapes and papaws, sweetens the persimmons which, until then, have puckered up the mouth like a drawstring. It curls back the bittersweet jackets, so that the brilliant berries gleam from wherever their vines have wandered, along the fences, or in the tops of trees. Country children have always earned pocket money by gathering and selling bittersweet and nuts in the fall, especially walnuts. For years, little Indiana boys went to school with hands and wrists dyed a rich dark brown which usually stayed, despite many frantic maternal scrubbings, until nearly Christmas.

In pioneer days the shade of brown commonly used for linsey-woolsey and jeans was derived from walnut leaves. Women colored the wool before it was spun, placing a layer of it in a large dye kettle, adding a layer of walnut leaves, repeating this process until the kettle was full, then covering the whole with spring water. After three days the wool was removed and inspected, and if not yet dark enough was returned to the kettle for a time. Colors obtained in this way were supposed to remain unaltered throughout the life of the fabric. The method gave us our familiar expression "*dyed in the wool*" to indicate fixity. Besides brown, the easiest shades to obtain from the woods were black and yellow (often from sumac berries and sassafras flowers) which is why the pioneers of Indiana were so often clothed in these three colors.

The wild harvests of woods and hills supplied settlers and Indians with many comforts and pleasures. Burdock burs were stuck together to form dolls and other small toys. Both white and Indian children used milkweed pods to form "birds," marking the eyes and wings with charcoal or dye, perching them on branches, using them in their play. Interesting and well loved "shuck dolls" were made from corncobs with the attached husks tied down and faces painted on; they were given bonnets and dresses, and sometimes cloth arms. Milkweed silk, from pods burst open by frost, was used to fill mattresses for the cradles of babies and dolls.

Women used sassafras to scent and refine their homemade

soap. And there were stories (handed down in our community) of girls who secretly tinted lips and cheeks with pale pink (much diluted) pokeberry juice, women who concealed gray hairs with a mild walnut stain.

Wild ginger and dried berries were used as flavoring in cooking. The great mullein, a tall and very stately plant, was sometimes made into candlewick or used as a torch. Pioneer women gathered many plants to make dyes, also to make medicinal teas (strawberry, peppermint, and bergamot leaves; camomile flowers; rose hips; wild ginger; sassafras bark) and harvested other medicinal plants to be used for common ills, many of which were quite serious. Of the homemade medicines of the early settlers it was said, laconically and probably very truthfully, that "some cured, some kilt."

My great-grandmother, an early-Indiana schoolteacher in her youth, had a great interest in folkways, and when I was a little girl, told me a great deal about the materia medica of Indiana pioneers, their treatments, superstitions, and axioms. (Her own mother had been one of those pioneer women who learned and did all they could to help the sick in their lonely, doctorless communities.)

One of the most interesting things she told me had to do with the controversial saying: "Feed a cold and starve a fever." It was a mistake, she said, for people to look upon this as a rule, for it was intended as a warning. The real meaning was: "Feed a cold and (you'll have to) starve a fever!"

The gathering of medicinal herbs, however, is by no means an abandoned pursuit. I know a couple in the Indiana hills, some twenty miles north of Cincinnati, who last summer gathered and sold to a crude-drug company enough ginseng to buy a new shotgun for the husband and a fur-trimmed coat for the wife. (Dealers buy ginseng for export to the Orient, where it is valued as a remedy for innumerable ills.)

The first fall after our squirrels were a year old, we decided to go into the woods and fill several bags with nuts for the winter meals of our furry pets, indoors and outdoors. I took my rifle for target practice, which usually meant shooting apples off the sycamore trees or crackers off thorn trees. Soon after we entered the woods, we came upon a nice stand of walnut trees, but found the ground bare and knew the squirrels had been there first.

"I'd eat a walnut myself, if I could get one," said Lee, squinting up at one of the trees.

"I'll bring one down for you," I offered, throwing a shell into the chamber of my gun.

"There's not even a stone here to crack it open," he pointed out.

"I'll open it for you," I promised rashly. Aiming with care, I squeezed the trigger and dropped a walnut—*in two precise halves!* It was the luckiest shot I ever made, a pure fluke of course, but Lee was much impressed, and I think even Bill would have considered it a triumph.

Gathering nuts was not as easy as one might think, for the squirrels carried them off almost as fast as they fell, and we had to get up early (sans pun) to outwit them. Walnuts were plentiful, but nuts from the shagbark hickories were less abundant, and good ones not easy to find. Many hickory nuts are wormy, and these the squirrels leave behind. Just because the ground is covered with nuts does not mean that you are in luck. It probably means that they are all rejects by the furry inspection crew.

Squirrels know instantly whether an unopened nut is good or bad, either by smell or weight, or perhaps by appearance. I have watched the wild squirrels discard or refuse hickory nuts that looked perfectly sound to me, but when I picked them up and cracked them open, I found, of course, that the squirrels were right and I was wrong.

Beechnuts are so tiny that much time is lost in gathering them, and often they are neither well filled nor good. Acorns are a favorite food of all squirrels but must be fed to pets with care, as too many are injurious to the kidneys. Butternuts are scarce in our part of the country, chestnuts not available at all except for the horse chestnut (buckeye), which is poison, as has been mentioned. This is a matter to be strongly stressed, however, because many children are allowed to play with them, and pets are encouraged to eat them. Some people insist that a buckeye carried in the pocket all winter will prevent "growing pains" and rheumatism and there are medical men who will tell you that this may be quite true—if the carrier really believes it.

The fairly large blue grapes which grow wild in Indiana have a delightful flavor. The small darker ones, hard and bitter and horribly sour, are called "fox grapes" because (Bill's theory) "only such a varmint as a fox could stand 'em."

Groany and Mimi liked the blue grapes, liked the taste of pawpaws mellowed by frost, and loved persimmons. But persimmons, being very messy, were quite offensive to my fastidious little Groany, and he would eat them only if he did not have to handle them. I would feed him small neat bites from the tip of my finger. Persimmon pulp may be very successfully frozen, and makes a delicious pudding. Wild animals, especially coons and possums, eat this pulp and discard the seeds, which are relished by hungry birds.

In the woods Lee and I watched that familiar autumnal conclave, the gathering of blackbirds, chattering and calling, so many alighting on a single tree that it appeared to be covered with black polka dots, then setting out in a sudden whirring flight, streaking across the sky in vast numbers.

Like everything else in the woods, they seemed to be gorging on the harvest bounty in preparation for the long winter. Birds were thick in cornfields and seed patches. Sometimes they ate so much that they could scarcely lift themselves from the ground and took off like a plane too heavily laden to gain altitude, barely clearing a fence.

Crows, too, were in the cornfield, and we never ceased to

find them fascinating. Bill had always objected to crow-shooting, believing that the harmful insects destroyed by these birds more than justified their existence, and that any creature so intelligent deserved special consideration.

It is entirely true, and not at all far-fetched, to say that crows have a hilarious sense of humor and play outrageous jokes on one another. They steal from one another for fun, and those who have been robbed steal their "goods" back again with triumphant shouts of what might be called laughter, since it is certainly an expression of mirth. They swoop down and tease farm animals and take great delight in scaring them. Bill called them "the caw-caw and haw-haw birds."

Tests have shown that crows have a number-sense up to a certain point. A sentinel who sees five hunters enter a building and watches them emerge one by one, will know when all have left. This number-sense belonged, in somewhat the same way, to the shepherds of biblical days who, at night, watched their animals pass under the rod or staff, and though unable to count, knew when any were missing. Crows are also able to tell the difference between a man carrying a gun and one carrying a stick.

Bill could identify every call of these birds. The "greeting" or passing call, low and brief, is exchanged between crows in flight, or offered to a newcomer. The "command" is a fairly low *c-a-w* given by a leader to his flock, and might be very accurately translated as, "Follow me!" There is a mourning call given on sighting dead companions, a love call "sung" during the courting dance of the male, a help call, such as a crow would utter while defending himself against an enemy like the red-tailed hawk, and hoping to hold out until the cavalry arrives. There is a fighting call which is a growling, snarling sort of sound—the sounds made by fighting crows and hawks are always a little horrifying. (Indeed, the wildest, most chilling, primordial sound I have ever heard was made by two red-tailed hawks screaming over a woods, one spring day, as they fought a desperate battle in the sky.)

Crows have a sense of morality, and treat each other with sympathy, kindness, and loyalty. If a crow is injured, the rest of the flock will respond to his distress calls, feed him, and try to carry him. If he dies, they mourn him with sorrowful laments.

It is well known that crows "hold court" with a great deal of noisy "testimony," appear to convict an evildoer, and afterward execute him by picking him to death. Bill was always irritated and somewhat hurt when city visitors doubted this story. "City folks," he said mournfully, "can tell you all about the ways of lions and elephants in Aferca—but they never read nothing about the ways of things in their own woods!"

The most common crow call, of course, is the sentinel's warning which alerts the entire woods, and is understood and respected by all birds and animals. In autumn the "passing call" is frequently heard as the birds go to and from the cornfields, feasting before the cold and sometimes hungry days of winter begin.

The flight of crows is the subject of a back-country "fortune-telling" verse:

One for sorrow,
Two for mirth,
Three for a wedding,
Four for a birth.

In fact, much folklore and many sayings are references to nature or to wildlife behavior. Some of the most familiar are:

"Cuter'n a coon on a limb"
"Happy as a jaybird in a full cherry tree"
"Dumb as a dove"
"Lazy as a cowbird"
"About as tasty as crick water"
"Mad as a hornet"

"Blind as a bat in daytime"

"Crazy as a hoot owl"

"Slower than a hoppy-toad"

"Skinny as a katydid"

"Sneaky as a varmint"

"Naked as a jaybird" (Refers to a newly hatched bluejay)

"Sour as a green persimmon" (Said of a person's disposition)

"Fair as a flitter" (A butterfly)

"Homely as a crawdad"

"Ugly as a mud turtle"

"No bigger'n a gnat"

"About as welcome as a polecat" (Skunk)

"I'd as soon walk into a hornet's nest!" (Said of a place of dissension)

"He wasn't knee-high to a grasshopper." (Very young or very small)

"Looks like she's clouding up to rain!" (Said of a girl about to cry)

"It stung me like a nettle!" (An insult)

"He was burning the wind!" (Moving with tremendous speed)

"She stuck to him like a bur."

A man whose small son accompanied him everywhere might introduce the child by saying, "This is my little stick-tight." (Stick-tights, flat seeds with sharp edges, stick to fur and clothing in the fall.)

One who is ailing might say, "I feel rough as a corncob!"

Several expressions from pioneer days are still glibly used in the back country, even though their origin has been completely forgotten. For example:

"It scared the wadding out of me!"

("Wadding" was the material stuffed against a charge of powder to hold it firmly in the breech of a muzzle-loading gun. Since, in an emergency, the fringes of a man's buckskins could be used as wadding, their function was more than merely decorative.)

". . . Stiff as a ramrod!"

(Still widely used, though few people who utter it could identify or explain the rigid metal, sometimes wooden, rod with which pioneers rammed a charge into a muzzle-loader.)

"I'll see what I can scare up for supper."

(This expression, commonly used by back-country housewives, originated in the days when a hearty meal depended upon "scaring up" and shooting game for the table.)

A "coon-track rain" is a very light drizzle, just enough to show the prints of a raccoon's feet on the ground.

A hard torrential rain is a "toad-strangler," or a "gully washer."

Among the sayings I have heard uttered philosophically by Bill or his cronies were:

"You have to take the briars with the roses."

"Where there's lightning, there's thunder."

"Dove without, weasel within."

"A buzzard won't eat a buzzard."

"Never bother a quiet snake."

"If you throw enough stones, you can fetch down any walnut."

"Never let the same bee sting you twice."

October is the favorite month of Indiana dreamers and of many others who know the woodlands, and probably no part of this tawny season is more moving, even to the most insensitive beholder, than the miracle of migration.

One still fall morning, after the singing of the insects had vanished and frost had come, I was walking along the street when overhead I heard a sound that, more than once, has brought me up from my sleep in the night, the unforgettable sounds of honkers leading their southward flight across the skies.

I stopped and looked up, and saw the wedge against the

morning skies. It was an enormous flight and took some time to pass and I watched it vanish into the distance, and felt lonely with its going. Then across the street I saw a man whose eyes had also followed the flight, an old farmer, his whiskers a white stubble, his hair gray curls on the back of his neck, hands gnarled with labor, face as crinkled and brown as a tobacco leaf. People had kept on walking, hurrying up and down, skirmishing with stop signs, turning right and left. But the old man and I had seen the wild geese fly, and a little nod and smile of understanding passed between us. So does a mutual love of nature and a mutual interest in the ways of wild creatures unite with sudden empathy persons of totally divergent personalities and backgrounds.

Sometimes it is possible to feel the same empathy with someone you have never seen at all, have never known and never will. I remember hearing a certain hunter talk about a skipper he had known when he was in the Navy, an old man pressed into service after retirement because there was a war and his skills and knowledge were needed. He was willing enough to contribute his skills and knowledge, but he loathed the highly mechanized ships of modern times.

"*I* know how to navigate," he complained. "I don't need all this junk. I can take this ship anywhere on the seas, anywhere you want me to go! *Just show me a star. . . .*"

I never heard this old man's name, but many an autumn night, as I looked up into the wheeling paths of Sirius and Orion and Aldebaran, I wished that I might have known him, this skipper who never heard of me, but with whom I shared a kinship just the same.

The crisp and smoky days of fall seemed to invigorate all woodland creatures. Mimi and Groany ran, skipped, hopped, and played from morning until night, even forgetting their afternoon naps. I watched their play many times and, as farfetched as it may sound (like so many things connected with these little animals), I came to believe that squirrels have imagination and play "pretend" games, especially when they are small.

Many times I have watched Groany slip cautiously past nothing-at-all, then run madly as if "it" were chasing him. On other occasions I have seen him creep very, *very* carefully up to a doorway, peep around it with a great show of caution, then dash forward, pounce upon "something," and appear to be worrying it.

He often played like a child, making little "houses" out of boxes or paper bags, going in and out and back in again, amusing himself in this way for hours. He sometimes established temporary quarters in a large paper bag placed on the floor, carried into it a "blanket" from his bowl (or purloined a hand towel instead), patted this into a neat bed, and took a nap there. One fall he slept in his paper bag for several nights and would have continued for several more, but the weather grew very hot, so I hid the bag. It gave him almost no air, as he was a very tiny object when curled up in the closed end of this great brown container.

(Even in the woods, such moving about is not unusual. A fox squirrel may have a permanent home in a tree cavity, but use a summer leaf nest and even another den or two at the same time.)

Whenever Mimi found something especially fascinating, such as a bright cuff link or earring, she would pick it up in her mouth with the intention of carrying it back to her bowl. However, if she saw me coming, she would slip the object back into her mouth, completely out of sight, and sit staring past me as though she had absolutely nothing to conceal. This air of extreme innocence betrayed her, just as it betrays a naughty child.

It is impossible, I have found, to forcibly remove an object from a squirrel's mouth. This something that must be accomplished by stealth or surprise.

Stealth: Offer the squirrel a more desirable object, such as a black walnut (whole), and he will drop the earring to take the food. The second object must be large, or he will take both in his mouth at once.

Surprise: Wait until the object is in plain sight. (Squirrels carry small items about halfway out of their mouths.) Then strike it suddenly with a sharp downward motion, so that it falls to the floor, but without striking the animal.

More than once, when I took something forbidden away from Mimi, she would sit and stare at me defiantly, then reach out her little hand and deliberately scratch me. She scratched like a kitten, with a petulant downward motion of the left hand, and made bright red marks on my arm. Lee thought this was very spirited and awfully cute.

When I ironed anything, she came running to play on the supports underneath the ironing board, swaying, swinging, doing somersaults as if on a trapeze. Even as a baby, she was given to daring gymnastic performances, and once when she jumped on a branch we had put in the little cage to encourage play, she caught it in her arms, went once around it, could not stop, but kept on revolving and squalling in fright.

One day she leaped up and caught the chain of the cuckoo clock which, from the effect of this added weight, slowly slid toward the floor with a grating sound. This startled Mimi and she leaped to the other chain, which also began to slide downward. While she was clinging for dear life, the clock struck twelve and the cuckoo came out, bobbing and calling over her head, until the chains reached the floor. This all but scared the furry daylights out of Mimi; indeed, it frightened her so much that she leaped upon *me* for protection (Lee being away at the time), hid behind my back, and peered over my shoulder to see whether this cuckooing monster was still pursuing her.

Sometimes when Lee got into bed, she would curl up beside him and lick his hand like a puppy, for ten or fifteen minutes. At other times he would put his hand on the bedside table and she would fall asleep there, with her head on his palm. Not wanting to disturb her, he would remain motionless as long as possible, usually until his arm was stiff and numb. Then at last, he would lift her and tuck her in at the foot of the bed, and she trusted him so completely that she did not even open an eye when he moved her, but remained a sleepy, cuddly, content little bundle of fur.

I know of but one other instance of such utter devotion and complete understanding between a human being and a little squirrel. In this case, the man was a monk, Father John, at an abbey in southern Indiana.

He had a pet squirrel named Bobby that he had found and brought up, and they shared many hours of happy companionship. Like all squirrels, Bobby loved a warm and cosy hiding place, and nothing could have been more pleasing to him than Father John's capuche, the pointed black hood that was a part of his monastic garb and hung down at the back of his neck when not being used to cover his head.

The capuche made an extremely comfortable retreat for Bobby when strangers came near, or when he was disturbed by unfamiliar sights and sounds. Also, he could peep out and see just what was going on, and huddle down out of sight again if what he saw did not please him.

Now and then Father John made a trip to a Catholic hospital at Evansville and carried his pet with him. While there, he took Bobby to the children's ward, where he told the children stories about him, and taught them how to play with him. After Bobby became accustomed to the children, he loved these trips and had all the play he wanted—a rare attainment for a squirrel.

All children love to watch squirrels and always want to feed them, but should never be allowed to feed them by hand. Since a squirrel's eyes are set unlike ours, he does not have the same range of vision. Sometimes he knows what he is eating, it seems, only by the smell and feel of it. To a squirrel, anything hard is probably a nut, and therefore to be bitten. For this reason, he is likely to bite a finger or fingernail, and a bite from a wild animal is a dangerous thing It is very unwise for any adult to offer a wild squirrel food from his hand, or to permit a child to do so.

However, Father John had no need to fear that his pet would injure a child, for Bobby had lost his teeth much as Mimi had lost hers, was unable to bite anything at all, and could eat only soft or ground food. In the hope of strengthening him, his owner gave him cod-liver oil and orange juice, one in a medicine dropper, the other in a small dish. He hated the oil and put up a valiant battle to avoid it, but loved the orange juice. I have heard of other squirrels that liked and wanted orange juice, though ours did not.

Once when Father John made a trip to town, carrying Bobby with him, he stopped in at an ice-cream parlor for a sundae. Bobby grew tired of waiting for him to finish this delicacy and began to squirm like a restless child, so the monk took him out of his pocket, perched him on his knee, and began to feed him some of the crushed nuts. A lady at the next table seemed startled by this unusual sight, so Father John explained the situation to her, and she laughed and said she was a reporter, and thanked him for giving her a good story. Later, her account of this little pet was published in her paper, with a cartoon of Father John leading the abbey band that was his pride and joy, while Bobby watched the whole procedure from the capuche.

Bobby regularly accompanied his owner on trips to nearby towns, and one day, while in Louisville, Kentucky, they attended a movie together. Father John bought tickets for the matinee, for himself and some children he was escorting, stopped in the lobby for bags of salted peanuts, then herded his charges into the crowded theater and sat down to enjoy the picture. Almost at once, however, he felt Bobby becoming restless and starting to move around. Suddenly the little squirrel thrust his head out and the monk was horribly certain that, at any moment, the lady in the next seat would see the little animal and start to scream.

Hastily he gave his pet some of the crushed peanuts, hoping to quiet him. It was the smell of these tasty tidbits that had roused Bobby in the first place, so he accepted them happily and retired to Father John's pocket to eat the crumbled pieces in seclusion.

For about three years this monk and his little pet were inseparable, and when at last Bobby died, there was a never-to-be-filled vacancy in the good man's heart. The other monks and priests and seminarians were full of sympathy for him after the loss of his pet and were pleased, one summer day, to hear that a nest of baby fox squirrels had been found on the grounds. The mother was gone and had not returned and it was assumed that she had been killed, for the hunting season had opened a few days earlier.

(In Indiana, legal squirrel hunting begins in August, a great mistake since there are babies still in the nest at this time. Squirrel hunting should be postponed until the small squirrels are old enough to care for themselves.)

The young seminarian who found the orphaned litter hastened to carry the news to Father John. "Several people have been asking for them," he said, "but we thought you should have the first choice. . . ."

Father John shook his head, and his words were an eloquent tribute to a beloved little comrade that could never be replaced.

"I thank you for thinking of me," he said, "but if you don't mind . . . just don't let me see them."

XII

Many winters are so severe that much suffering is brought upon the little woods animals, especially the squirrels. One particular winter, food was very scarce because the mast had been so poor that fall. Excessive summer heat had burned and withered many of the wild fruits that birds and animals normally eat during the cold months, and the nut crop had failed.

Also we had one of the worst ice storms in our history. It had rained heavily, a sleet storm followed, and a tremendous burden of ice began to form over the entire countryside. Every tree, branch, twig, bush, and stump was covered by this thick and heavy coating. In the towns and villages and on the farms it shrouded the rooftops and chimneys, the window sills, porches, steps, radio aerials, and TV antennas. Fences and poles and tree trunks had a covering like a transparent glaze on a cake.

This formation of ice was so thick that it resembled pure crystal. Trees and bushes seemed carved of it, cut with facets that gleamed and sparkled when the wind moved them. To anyone who has never witnessed such a thing, an ice storm is incredibly beautiful, but to persons familiar with its dangers, it is less enchanting.

I was doing volunteer work in a mental hospital at the time and was just turning into the hospital grounds when it appeared that the whole winter world was beginning to shatter under its insupportable load of ice. First there came a faint and terrifyingly familiar sound, a light musical tinkling, as delicate as fairy bells far off, the sound of ice breaking. Then there was a sharp snapping as a twig fell from a tree. Another twig fell, and another, and many more. Suddenly whole limbs began to rip away from trunks and fall with a terrible shattering sound as ice and wood came down together. The hospital grounds were full of large trees, and ice-covered branches began to collapse on all sides. Just as I turned into the north drive, a huge elm split apart with a hideous crash, half of it falling across the drive right in front of my car, just like in the movies.

I backed hurriedly away and took another drive leading to the office. There the director told us that all volunteer work had been canceled for the rest of the day, and all cars were to be removed from the grounds immediately.

The trip home was one of the most frightening things I ever experienced. On all sides, trees, poles, and fences were collapsing, one after the other, as though suddenly struck down by some mighty, petulant giant. Along every street, great limbs and branches and trees were toppling with a shattering noise of crashing wood and splintering ice. Poles went down, narrowly missing cars and carrying dangerous wires with them. Bushes split apart, shrubs collapsed like kindling. The ice storm reached for miles, leaving toppled poles and fences and shattered branches all across the state, destruction that was not unlike the wake of a tornado. Beautiful shade trees many years old lay uprooted on the lawns of farmhouses, in ice-covered fields, and over broken fences. It was possible to drive for miles in the country and see every utility pole lying flat.

Storms of such severity are not common, but even mild ice storms bring great suffering to wildlife, as do heavy snows and driving blizzards. Bill used to talk about the tragedy that might overtake coveys of quail during such a season. Quail, he explained, roost on the ground in what appears to be adequate cover, arranged in a sleeping circle with their tails together and their heads out, alert to any approaching enemy. If such a storm comes, they huddle together, waiting for this new enemy to pass while the heat from their bodies melts the cold. But if the ice is extremely heavy, they may be entirely covered and perish under this impenetrable coating of death.

During hard winters when food is scarce, squirrels have to come out of their dens to forage on the ground. Sometimes, however, the layer of snow and ice is so thick that they are unable to dig through it to buried nuts. If ice coats their den trees meanwhile, they cannot climb back up to their nests again, and are trapped on the ground, where they usually fall prey to prowling foxes, raccoons, owls, and red-tailed hawks.

Other wild creatures are also trapped on the ground, as Marjorie often discovered. During such storms, she and her husband and two young sons supplied food for birds and animals in the woods, and watched for any that might be in distress. Once Denny, her younger son, found a beautiful cock pheasant, decorated with brilliant paint-box colors, trapped in a snowdrift, helpless and half frozen.

Denny managed to release him, but the bird was so exhausted from his struggles and lack of food, and so weakened by exposure, that he seemed near death. Denny therefore lugged him home, and Marjorie—quite accustomed to such unexpected guests and fully prepared for them—established him in a cage in the basement, where he grew warm and was soon eating voraciously. When he was well enough to march around and loudly demand his release, they sent him back to the snowy woods, now made more tenable by a rise in temperature and a few days of sunlight.

Such bright winter days are perfect for rabbit hunting, for it is then that rabbits emerge to warm themselves in the sun. No respectable hunter, however, would "shoot a rabbit settin," as it is considered both unsporting and unprincipled not to give him a chance to run for his life. Since his speed is about thirty miles per hour, killing him requires some fast work with a shotgun.

Rabbits are not hunted in thick woodlands, but are found in fields, meadows, and other open spaces. On very cold days they are "holed up" under thick brush, but one kick at a brush pile may bring out four or five. If the countryside is hilly, the hunter takes note and acts accordingly, for a rabbit always runs uphill.

The first shotgun I ever had was a little twenty-gauge Stevens single shot. It was too long for my arms, though, so Bill removed the recoil pad, cut the stock to fit me, and replaced the pad. Some of his cronies said this would ruin the balance of the gun, but it didn't. In fact, I always had the rather eerie feeling (probably because I was so young) that this gun was "enchanted," because I never once shot it without hitting my target.

A shotgun can have a tremendous kick, and should never be used by an uninstructed person. Since I am small, the kick of a twelve-gauge, double-barrel shotgun can turn me completely around. Bill advised me to use a lighter gun, and taught me how to hold it so that my shoulder took the recoil without being hurt. One of my favorite guns was a smooth, light, beautiful .410 Marlin which Lee gave me years later for my birthday. Bill had assured me many times that *every* Marlin was a thing of beauty and a joy forever.

It was very interesting to me to find that there are certain codes of conduct learned, observed, and passed on by generations of respected Indiana hunters, the breed to which Bill belonged, and which have never been put down in writing. I write them now as he taught them to me:

You never borry nor lend a gun. (Asking to borry a feller's gun is second only to asking to borry his wife . . . or his hunting-dog.)

If you invite a feller to hunt with you, it is only polite to let him have the first shot at whatever game gets up.

If you get game and your friend don't, it'd be a plumb insult for you to say to him, "On account of you didn't get none, I'll divide with you." Nope, you say something like, "You would do me a favor if you'd take home a few of these rabbits. I'll have more'n I can do, to get *three* of them cleaned!"

Two hunters never shoot at the same game. If one shoots and gets game, that's his business. If he *misses*, it's his business. *You* hold your fire and let him have his own chance. Because if two fellers shoot at once, who knows which one killed it? Even between old cronies, this could cause a wallop of a ruckus!

It's all right to hold a feller's gun for him while he climbs a fence, but outside of that, keep your hands off of it unless you first ask him, "Mind if I take a look at it?" You don't pick up and prod and poke a feller's firearm any more'n you'd pick up and prod and poke one of his childern!

If you see a man's gun is rusted, barrel pitted and blueing all wore off, hunt with somebody else. Because a feller that don't take care of his gun is good-for-nothing in other ways, too. *Never hunt twice* with a feller that mistreats his gun or his dog, takes more than the limit or more than he can use, shoots game and then throws it away, drinks while he hunts, kills just to be killing, or wounds something and then don't track it down and put it out of its misery. *He's no better'n a weasel!*

When you invite a man to rabbit-hunt with you, it's polite for you to hunt the low ground and let him have the high. Because (on account of the way a rabbit runs) whoever is on the hills will have the best chance at it.

When a hunter runs out of ammunition and asks to borry from you, you're duty-bound to share with him, even if he's just a stranger you met in the woods. But he don't have to pay it back, and you oughtn't to expect it.

If you shoot and miss, there's no reason to feel bored (embarrassed) over it, because that's the way of things. *Nobody hits nothing every time!* So just keep still—instead of shaming yourself by saying the cartridges are loaded uneven, or the gun pulls to the right, or the sun was in your eyes. Don't never think folks is so dumb that they don't know fool-talk when they hear it!

If an old-time hunter meets a kid (in the woods or out of it) who has a real-for-true interest in hunting and the outdoors, it's his place, his *obligation* you might say, to teach this kid all he knows about guns and game and the ways of nature, and to take him hunting. ("Even," Bill would add, with a sly look at me, "if he happens to be a girl!")

When you meet another hunter in the woods, it's unfriendly not to speak, no matter if he's a stranger to you. Just nod and say, "How'd do!" or, "Any luck?"—something like that. But don't talk loud, and don't stand and gab, or you'll scare off the game and not get any.

Never hunt where another feller has already started unless he invites you. Find a range of your own.

There is an old superstition lingering in the remote hills of southern Indiana which says: *Never let a woman touch your gun.* Bill told me this came into our state with the Pennsylvania Dutch settlers, and had its origin in their belief that if a witch put a spell on a firearm, it would never shoot straight again.

It was interesting to observe the hunters, hear their talk, learn to know them as individuals. Some, I found, were called "shiftless" and "do-less" for the same reason that such terms were applied to Jim Riley, the boy, whose days idled away amid the fascinations of nature became stepping stones to his fame as James Whitcomb Riley, the poet.

These particular hunters seemed to spend their lives groping through woods and hills with a sense of emptiness never to be filled. Years later, my mother-in-law taught me a sad old-country saying which was a poignant reminder of them: "*He hears the bell, but he doesn't know where.*" With guidance and education some of these men, I feel, would have become inspired naturalists, historians, geologists, botanists, writers, wildlife photographers, foresters.

But all were quiet-mannered men, kindly, openhearted, generous in deed and spirit, whose friendly rivalry never became malicious competition, and who were utterly devoid of sham. Their simple honesty impressed me deeply and has been strongly responsible, I think, for my dislike of pretension in any form.

(Even in the quaint repast known as "brunch" which is something, I have observed, that most women neither mention nor give, except when putting on airs. I once attended the meeting of a fund-raising committee called to plan a civic breakfast, though this commonplace term was viewed with considerable alarm. One woman kept saying over and over, "It would be a great deal more chic if we announced a brunch!"

"Tell you what," I finally answered, thinking of Bill, "let's be chic-er than all getout, and announce a brupper!")

During the cold winter months, Bill ate a great deal of rabbit stew (which I could never bring myself to taste) and, worse still, rabbit hash.

"Well, I guess *some* folks think it's good," he would tell me, "or there wouldn't be a town named after it!" (And there *is* a town called Rabbit Hash, in Kentucky.)

Because of his fondness for this dubious dish, he spent many winter days tracking down the basic ingredient, and I liked going with him, for rabbit-hunting is a very conversational sport. There is no need to be wary and silent, as in hunting other game, and hunters may exchange information, observations, experiences, even confidences in companionable talk.

Rabbit-hunting in Indiana can be a very dangerous sport, however, for "average hunters" are shooting at everything that moves (especially on the first day of the season) and there are frequent accidents.

I had a heart-stopping experience once, during this hunting season. I had been in the woods, filling some feeding stations for Bill, and was cutting across a field to get back to the house. It was a beautiful winter day, bright and cold, with snow on the hills and hunters in the valleys. I am not very tall, and as I crossed the field, I was in weeds over my head.

Suddenly I heard the sound of voices, and a party of hunters came over the hill, men with shotguns. I shouted, but the wind was in my face and they did not hear me, and of course they could not see me. I knew that if I tried to get out of range they would see the weeds moving, and somebody would shoot. Very slowly, I slid to the ground and lay there, making myself as flat as possible, hoping (as I heard their guns blast) that the rabbits were not running my way. I have never been more frightened, and I know just how the wild things feel as they huddle against the earth with hunters around them, their sense of relief when the men have passed on and they are safe.

As we walked through the snow on winter days, Bill would identify all sorts of tracks, show me how a fox had run down a rabbit, where a hawk had pounced upon a squirrel or a pheasant, where coons and wood mice and weasels had run. I learned a few of the tracks, but never became skilled at it, and often mistook the footprint of a dog for the track of a fox.

In the Lick Creek hills, Bill had once found the track of a wildcat, and while this was uncommon in our part of Indiana, it was not really astonishing. This animal (known as the bobcat because of his "bobbed" tail) lives in and around the area where Illinois and Kentucky join the southwestern tip of Indiana. Now and then, a roaming wildcat moves north and takes up residence for a brief time in some region where he has easy access to rabbits, squirrels, birds, and poultry yards. This has happened, both winter and summer, in our part of the state.

In pioneer days the forests of Indiana were alive with wildcats, but that was long ago, and now Indiana people know so little about this animal that rumors of his presence can create a near panic in our community. Every unusual sound is attributed to the wildcat. People call the newspapers to report roars, growls, howls, coughs, screams, groans, and wails, and keep a sharp eye open for the intruder. However, a wildcat is not easily seen, inasmuch as he is a nocturnal animal, and also because he makes his home in very secluded places—remote hills, tangled underbrush, wooded swamps, thickets, and sheltered dens.

Cat-like, he is very curious, and often so busy stopping to examine interesting objects and places that his zigzag track in the snow appears wandering and aimless. When traveling fast, he may move in leaps as long as ten feet.

A wildcat does not roar or cough or howl. His cries usually resemble the yowls, whines, and meows of the familiar house cat, but at times he does utter high and rather blood-curdling screams. My great-grandmother told me stories (heard from *her* great-grandmother) about the cries of wildcats echoing through the great Indiana wilderness at night, and how often pioneer children were frightened by this sound.

When I was a little girl, farmers living two or three miles east of my grandfather's house began to find partly eaten carcasses of cottontails, possums, and chickens, and to hear commotions around the poultry yards at night. There were reports, too, of terrified dogs that growled into the darkness, dashed into the house, and would not go out again.

One man shakily related that he had gone out late at night to fill a water bucket at the pump, and as he glanced up he saw, in the bright moonlight, a great streaked-and-spotted cat watching him curiously. As he turned, it growled at him, he said, and he threw the bucket at it and fled into the house.

One day in early summer my father had to make a call at a farm some miles away, and took my sister Virginia along. She was about six then, a chubby, alert little girl with curly hair and large, all-seeing eyes. When they returned that evening, she was full of excited talk about the trip.

"I saw ducks on a pond," she reported, "and two sheeps fighting . . . and a mother bird carrying a worm . . . and a baby colt nursing its supper . . . *and a bear looking out of its house!*"

"A bear?" I echoed, scornfully. "Where?"

She described an old log cabin, long deserted, which stood close beside the road.

"The window was open in his upstairs," she insisted, "and he was looking out . . . *and he looked at us!*"

At this I shouted with ribald laughter, and so did my sister Mary Rose. Virginia began to cry, and my grandmother ordered me to hush—but the incident was not closed.

A little later the farmer who owned this place shot a wildcat as it was fleeing into the cabin. Evidently it had been living there for some time, hunting at night, and hiding in the loft. The loft window was open, and no doubt the animal had many times watched passers-by with the interest and curiosity of all wild things.

Of course, it is rare indeed for an Indiana farmer to be called upon to shoot a wildcat, but most people who live in out-of-the-way places keep at least one gun handy for use in country emergencies.

Marjorie had a light single-shot rifle which her boys had bought for target practice, and the first time I ever saw her shoot this gun, only our close friendship kept me from rolling on the ground with hilarious abandon. It was entirely too long for her, and in her innocence, she had learned to shoot it by balancing the stock *on top of her shoulder*, rearing backward until she could squint along the barrel and, through some sort of convulsive contortion, clutch the trigger just below her eye. What was even more staggering, she sometimes hit things, and once shot a mud turtle through the head when she found it trying to catch and drown and eat the birds that went to her pond to drink.

Still, I told her I had never seen anything so funny outside the pages of *Vogue*. A number of magazines, especially those dedicated to the *haute couture*, like to picture "country casuals" on models carrying or aiming guns. I used to save these pages to show Bill, spreading them out on his little old-fashioned round kitchen table, while he put on the steel-rimmed spectacles and inspected them with guffawing disbelief. We rocked with laughter over the way a haughty model handled her shotgun, speculated joyously over whether she would most likely be kicked in the jaw by the recoil, or blow the seat out of the pants of her escort, who stood nearby in impeccable tweeds and, judging from the proximity of the barrel, not long for this world.

Bill was honestly baffled as to why any magazine would suggest wearing "good goods to the woods," where the tweed skirt would soon be full of burs and stick-tights, the beautifully tailored jacket ripped apart by briars and whipped ragged by branches.

"Those pictures are not to be taken literally," I explained. "They're what might be called symbolic. The clothes show that the people are fashionable, and the guns indicate that they're rich enough to have a shooting box in Scotland."

Bill eyed me over his glasses.

"What in tarnation is a shooting box in Scotland?"

"If we *knew*," I told him, "we wouldn't care!"

When we went to the woods on icy winter days wearing our "country casuals," we looked like a perambulating rummage sale. In fact, we wore as much wool as we could carry and still walk upright, but none of the garments were new or fancy, and all were light in weight, so as not to tire us, or cause us to perspire once we had been warmed by walking. I saw Bill far less often in winter, but knew that no matter how biting the cold or how deep the snow, he made such trips every day to leave food for wildlife that might otherwise die of hunger.

Squirrels deprived of adequate food during such hard winters become weak and undernourished and are susceptible to scabies, a skin ailment caused by a small infectious mite. Those who suffer from this ailment, which is brought on by malnutrition, lose their fur, develop a mangy appearance, and sometimes have patches of skin entirely bare.

In our town many people regularly provide food for birds and animals during harsh winter months, and for that reason, town squirrels have a better chance to find food than do those in the woods. Yet even the town squirrels suffered greatly from malnutrition during the winter of the heavy ice storm, and their suffering was increased by the misunderstanding of persons who observed their unusual appearance, considered them carriers of some sort of plague, and drove them away or even killed them.

One man saw an almost naked squirrel, and coming to the common misinformed conclusion that anything different about an animal's appearance means rabies, immediately shot the little fellow.

We began to notice that many of the squirrels coming to our feeder showed symptoms of scabies. Almost all had naked patches of skin, and one little male was completely bare on the right side of his body.

I bought a liquid vitamin preparation from our veterinarian, and spread it on all the food put out for these squirrels. They ate it heartily, especially the little male, and before long we saw the new fur was growing on his bare side. All our wild squirrels dined on vitamins that year, and when spring came none were missing. In fact, there were a few additions to our usual callers, and all had splendid coats. The symptoms had disappeared.

Squirrels in the woods who suffer this disease of malnutrition often infect healthy ones and no doubt many die, especially if the sick squirrels enter their nests.

Marjorie used to watch a certain den in a tree just beyond her kitchen window, and had seen the squirrel who "owned" it spring out and chase callers away more than once. Squirrels are always possessive about their homes and resent pilfering intruders. However, Marjorie saw this same squirrel admit one that was obviously very ill, and so weak he could scarcely climb the tree.

During the dark winter months, squirrels go into a sort of semi-hibernation. Ours were lethargic, stayed in their bowls, and drowsed most of the day, but when spring came, they were as lively as ever. (Throughout their lives, activity was followed by complete rest. If they played hard one day, they would be very quiet the next.)

We always hoped we might have baby squirrels to observe, and thought Mimi would make a fine mother, for certainly no animal could have been more solicitous toward little ones than was Mimi toward her brothers. Naturalists consider the female squirrel a good mother who is devoted to her children and gives them unusually tender care.

However, the veterinarian at the museum of natural history told us that fox squirrels seldom mate in captivity, and did not encourage our hopes.

Nevertheless, the voice of nature persuaded both Groany and Mimi to prepare for the mating season. Mimi began to drink more water than usual, and ate a tremendous amount of food. Her appetite increased notably around Christmas time; she seemed utterly ravenous and demanded food all day, probably an instinct based on an unrealized anticipation of long weeks in the nest with young.

At any rate, Mimi was as fat as a little cookie jar through December and January. Then her appetite decreased and she gradually lost weight until she became quite thin. Her impulse to overeat did not reappear until months later.

As he came into the mating season, Groany grew nervous, irritable, cross, and finally belligerent. Sometimes he would refuse to allow Lee or Jamie to cross a room, but would stand in the middle of it, feet braced for a charge, lip snarling. They would call to me, in a great dither, "Come and get your little monster! We can't get out of the house. . . ."

I rocked with laughter, watching this small furry Horatius holding the bridge of his defiance against two full-grown adults. When he saw me coming, he screamed in angry protest, kicked and squalled and struggled when I snatched him up, but he would not bite me. No matter how much he resented what I did or how furious he might be, he never made the first antagonistic move toward me.

When he threatened Lee and Jamie, he meant business, and once or twice when they tried to pass him anyway, he very promptly charged them and nipped their ankles sharply. However, we had no fear of rabies, as he had never been near any animal except Mimi, who was as innocent as he of this affliction.

At the time of the mating season I observed that his genitals were inflamed and appeared sore, perhaps from scratching, as he seemed very uncomfortable and apparently suffered a good deal of itching, so I decided to take him to the animal hospital for an examination.

The doctor picked him up gently and looked at him, saying that he might be having some urinary infection. Groany seemed quiet, neither nervous nor afraid, but when the doctor started to examine him, he suddenly stiffened. His head went back, his eyes closed spasmodically, and he appeared to be gasping for air. The doctor quickly laid him down and began rolling him back and forth. I heard him say, "Now, now! Don't, little fellow, *don't!*"

I saw with horror that Groany was going into shock. Immediately I snatched him up and held him against my shoulder (where he had felt safe ever since babyhood), breathed into his mouth, and began talking to him. He relaxed so quickly that I thought he had died until I saw that his eyes were opening and felt his heart returning to normal. I stroked his fur, talked to him, carried him out to the car, and sat there holding him for some time. When at last he reached up for me to whisper to him, I knew he was all right.

"I'll never take you to a hospital again," I whispered. "I promise you, I *never* will."

Mimi, little baggage that she was, might be terrified, but she would fight to the bitter end. Against real terror, however, Groany's strength deserted him.

When I got him home again and put him back in his cage, I treated him with a pad of cotton dipped in cool water mixed with plain baking soda, about one teaspoon of soda to a quart of water. As I laid him down on his resting shelf, I slipped this pad under him. The coolness soothed the inflammation and the soda water relieved the itching discomfort. It was an excellent remedy and I used it for him whenever he came into another mating season.

Each year our pets became more tame—and more spoiled. Groany would even climb into his bowl and wait for me to come and cover him up, settling down with little *mm . . . mm . . . mm*'s of pleasure as I tucked him in. Both would come to us and "ask" in ways we now understood for whatever they wanted—to eat, to drink, to play, or perhaps to be scratched. They liked us to scratch their ears and jowls, under their chins, and at the base of their tails, which they could not reach. Groany loved to have his chest scratched and would stretch out his arms to give the scratcher more room.

Even as time passed and they grew to be five years old, many of their childhood interests remained with them. They had never ceased to be attracted to music, and we observed them carefully to see whether there were any types of music which had a special appeal for them. The results were highly entertaining.

Groany, the fastidious and elegant little gentleman, liked "better" music, and listened to it as though spellbound. There was an evening radio program from Cincinnati called "Music for You" (classical and semi-classical) which was his favorite, and when it came on, Groany would settle down into his blankets with his chin propped on the rim of his bowl and listen without as much as moving, in a solemn and introspective manner hilarious to watch. When it was time to hear "Music for You," one of us would say to the other, "Go and turn on the Philosopher's program." Soft and dreamy music seemed to fill him with quiet appreciation, and anyone who saw him would be moved to declare that he looked actually meditative.

Mimi, on the other hand, was a born hillbilly, and all hillbilly music attracted her attention, as did rock and roll. The better the beat, the better she liked it, the more eagerly she listened, and it was while we were tuned in on "You Don't Have to Be a Baby to Cry" that we heard her sing.

At least, we never knew what else to call it! In the midst of this number, she began to make a crooning sound we had never heard before. At first we were alarmed, thinking something was wrong with her. The sound was a little like the *crrr-onnnk* of her childhood, only softer and more prolonged. It was very reminiscent of the *crrrrrrrrrr* of pet hens, but had a humming, crooning quality difficult to describe.

Although this was a most astonishing development, it was some time before we told our veterinarian about it. We thought it most likely that he already considered us touched—bringing in stories about squirrels holding hands, knocking on doors, understanding English, watching TV, and sleeping in bed with us. *Singing yet!* We agreed that it might be too much for him.

But he was not too surprised when he finally heard about it, for members of the rodent (gnawing) family sing quite commonly. Mice sing, and naturalists tell us that, in spring, chipmunks sing together and birds come to listen. Nor is it unusual to hear raccoons singing on moonlit nights, especially in the fall. The old hunters used to laugh and say, "That coon ain't much on singing yet, is he? Must be a baby just learning how!" They were amused in the same way by baby owls trying to hoot. And on a farm, nothing is funnier than the discordant voice of a young rooster trying to crow like his elders.

That year, at the beginning of the mating season, Mimi's appetite had increased so much that she was no longer content with her tiny breakfast. Her one grape was now only the first course, and after she rode to the kitchen on Lee's shoulder, she had a breakfast like Groany's, a piece of apple, a nut, and a bit of lettuce.

I had always served both of them at the same time, putting their identical plates into their identical cages at identical moments. But one morning while I was still asleep, Lee went out to the kitchen, made the coffee, and fed the squirrels himself.

Because of his favoritism toward Mimi, I suppose, he gave her her breakfast first. When at last he prepared Groany's plate and put it in the cage, Groany would not have it. Haughtily he turned his back, ignored the food, ignored Lee, and was through with him forever!

Later, when Lee made conciliatory advances toward him, as he did many times, Groany charged him and tried to bite him. *Never again* did Groany play with him, sit on his knee, or share his cornflakes, and I had to admit that Mr. Dubbs really knew what he was talking about.

Mimi went through her usual cycle of eating, growing plump, losing her appetite, and becoming thin again. However, she did not seem as lively as usual and spent a great deal of time lying quietly in her bowl, or curled up under the bedspread on Lee's bed.

Ever since her struggle with pneumonia, she had suffered periodically with rhinitis, a nasal inflammation, but the veterinarian in charge at the museum of natural history (whom we consulted when our own doctor was away) had prescribed nose drops which seemed to control this ailment. Lee usually put these drops in her nose, and she was very patient about it, as long as it was he who did it. The rhinitis bothered her at times during the winter, but it was now spring, and the winter was past.

Lee, too, noticed that she did not seem well; indeed, she tried to tell him so. When he went to bed, she would follow him, climb to the bedside table, lay her head in his open hand as though to show him how miserable she felt, and murmur the plaintive little sound they always made when they were ill, "*Mmmmmmmmmmmm . . . mmmmmmmmmmmmm m. . . .*"

One night I heard a new sound, a small and desperate deathly-sick retching. It was Mimi. A veterinarian had once told me that animals belonging to the rodent family could not vomit—but Mimi could, and did. Yet when the nausea had passed, she seemed well enough, except that she was rather weak. Later that night, though, I caught her doing something that chilled me. She was trying to hide.

In animals, as in humans, there are certain age-old behavior patterns recognized as symptoms of approaching death. A man may pick at the covers and turn his face to the wall. Animals often try to hide away and die alone.

We called our veterinarian, but he had gone out of town and could not be reached; so early next morning, Lee telephoned for an appointment with the staff doctor at the museum of natural history, several miles away.

It was a beautiful spring day, so warm that the windows were open, but Mimi shivered and seemed cold. Hastily, we dressed, wrapped her in a small blanket, stroked her and talked to her reassuringly, and laid her in her covered basket. Then I heard a sound that filled me with cold apprehension—Chico, the little dog in the house next door, was howling a death howl.

In all his life he had never howled—not until now. I told myself it was my back-country upbringing amid so many superstitions and "signs" that made me afraid for Mimi when I heard this sound, nothing rational or logical, nothing to worry about.

When the veterinarian saw her, in the office of his own hospital, he said only, "You have a very sick little pet," but there was a finality in his voice which gave us little hope for her. He did not know, he told us, exactly what was wrong with her or what to do for her, but he thought the medicine he was giving us would relieve her—at least, for a time. Then he handed Lee a creamy bottle and told us to start it as soon as we got her home.

Mimi was very quiet all the way back, and Lee looked half ill with worry over her. As soon as we reached home, he carried her in and opened her basket. In the midst of her clean terry blankets, Mimi lay like a soft, bright little cuddle-toy, her head down on her small fists, her plumy tail spread over her back, her eyes closed, and when Lee gently began to lift her out, he found that she was dead.

We were all heartsick about Mimi, but to Lee losing her was almost like losing a child, for she had been his constant and devoted little companion every moment that he was at home, and there was an unusual love and rapport between them.

As the memory of a beloved pet never ceases to haunt its owners, so Mimi haunted us. We awoke in the morning to think of her perched on the bedside table eating her one grape. We saw her resting elegantly in her lamp bowl, one arm hung languidly over the rim. When lightning flashed at night, we remembered how she had feared it, and how Lee used to rescue her and take her back to bed with him to comfort her.

We put away her cage and her bowl and the little cup from which she had drunk ice water and sips of Coca-Cola poured from Lee's glass. There was no longer a stubborn little lump under the best bedspread, stealing a siesta in a forbidden place. No happy little figure leaped up to greet Lee at night with reaching arms and a welcoming, "*Mm . . . mm . . . mmmm.*" No little pet told him good night and curled up trustingly at his feet, dismissing me with a sharp "*Kack!*" Only her ghost remained to us, a poor substitute for the warm and lively little body, the bright and loving little spirit.

Groany was bewildered by her disappearance. Every morning he sat up and leaned far out of his bowl, looking and looking for her cage, for a glimpse of this little companion who had been with him all his life. We could see that he missed her, hunted for her, was lonely without her, and many days passed before he ceased to look for her.

We buried her beside Shad, and I remembered how the little dog Chico had howled that morning, and was no longer howling when we came back. I remembered, too, that the howling of a dog at the time of death is not merely a superstition, but a phenomenon observed for centuries by people of all lands and cultures. Even early Indiana settlers believed, when their dogs howled, that an Indian or some animal was dying in the forest not far away.

I first heard the peculiar howl of a dog in the presence of death when I was a little girl. It was a winter night, with a brilliant white moon and blue shadows on the snow; and over the countryside, farmhouses like ours were quiet and dark. But from my upstairs window I could see a light still burning in the distant house across the fields where old Considerate Mercer lay dying.

"They say he'll not last out the night," my grandmother told my grandfather at suppertime.

I thought of the biblical verse I had heard in church about "Death on a pale horse" and was afraid. If Death came for old Considerate Mercer tonight, he'd have to come by the one and only road, the road past our house. I remember how I left the window and hid my face in my pillow because I didn't want to see Death and his pale horse go by. And all the time, through the cold winter stillness, from all the way across the snowy fields, I could hear the faithful Mercer dog howling, howling.

Death was a figure dark and sinister, I thought, who wore rusty black funereal clothes and had a horrible skull where his face should have been. And when he galloped back on his bony white horse at daylight, Considerate Mercer would be tied on behind him, eyes wide with terror, crying out to us for help as he passed.

But, no, Death couldn't be like that, for Death healed all sorrow, my grandmother said. So he must be something like Considerate himself, a lively man who had a pleasant face and a kindly way with children. Considerate always knew funny riddles and stories to tell us, and magic tricks to surprise us. He'd shake out his red bandana handkerchief, show us it was empty, and *then* pull out of it willow whistles or stick candy for us to keep.

Yes, surely Death was a friendly man in a fine white suit and a tall white hat, and he and Considerate would ride past laughing and talking like a pair of old cronies, and maybe Considerate would shake the red bandana, show that it was empty, and then pull out of it, for his new friend, an extry-nice cigar.

It was then, on that night, that I first heard the death-howl, like an eerie cry of anguish, and I heard it again on the day Mimi died. Perhaps it was true, I thought, that Chico had howled because he sensed death—but it was such a *little* death. . . .

Only Groany was left to us now, he who had been the

smallest and frailest of all our pets; and since he was so lonely, Jamie and I spent a lot of time playing with him. (He still would not play with Lee.) At first we wondered whether Mimi might have had an illness that would infect him, but his health seemed perfect, and he was active and merry.

Mimi died in May. The following October I was ill, and while I was convalescent, but still in bed, Groany stayed with me much of the time, lying on the coverlet beside me, holding my hand. We often took naps together in this way. At night I carried him to his bowl and tucked him in.

One night, after he had been in bed for about an hour, I was startled by an unexpected and terrifying sound. I leaped up and rushed to him and found him retching as Mimi had retched. When Lee came out to see what had happened, I was crying bitterly.

"He's sick just like Mimi," I told him. "He's going to die in the same way. . . ."

We gave him some of the creamy mixture in a medicine dropper and he took it without protest. For a while it seemed to help him, but he grew nauseated again, became sicker and weaker. The next day I saw what I had been watching for and dreading. He was trying to hide.

We telephoned the veterinarian, who said he knew nothing else to do for him, but to keep trying the medicine. All of us realized how little has been discovered about the illnesses of wild animals. I lifted Groany upon my bed and stroked him and tried to comfort him, and he hid his face under the sleeve of my robe.

That night he was worse, and very weak. Lying on a little blanket beside me, he was still holding tight to me, his little hands clutching my fingers. Even then it seemed to me that I had never seen a more beautiful, more immaculate, more perfect little animal, his soft fawn coat, his pale beige vest and little beige socks, his fluffy combed-and-brushed tail.

I felt when I looked at him that he was close to death, and

perhaps, without knowing the nature of death, he felt it, too. For using his last bit of strength, he held up his little head for me to whisper to him. With tears falling down my face and glistening on his soft fur, I told him the time had come when we must leave each other, but I would never forget him, and I would always love him. He clung to my shoulder, as he had done when he was little and afraid, and toward morning he died.

Many tears have fallen into those tiny graves in the woods, not only through a sense of loss and grief, but also in sorrow because we knew nothing to do for our pets, nothing that would ease their suffering, nothing that would save their lives.

XIII

A few weeks later, Vera told me that Bushy had developed the same symptoms and died in the same way.

We were indeed lonely without the merry little sprites which, for more than five years, had enlivened our days and gladdened our lives. A tame squirrel is the dearest and most loving of pets, and it is significant that no person who ever had one and lost it, is able to speak of it without tears in his eyes, no matter how many years have passed since that day.

A squirrel is not easily obtained, however, and unless it is acquired when a baby, before it is weaned, it will probably never be tame. Of course, most squirrels *are* acquired during babyhood, especially in the hunting season after their mothers have been killed. But even if you find, rescue, and raise an orphaned squirrel, you are permitted to keep it, under Indiana law, only if you are granted a state permit or purchase a state license. Any squirrel held without one or the other is being held illegally, and likely to be seized by the county conservation officer (known, in the days before his resplendent uniform, as the "game warden").

The story of such a squirrel, a little fellow held illegally and subsequently seized, was brought to my attention by a teacher whom I will call Mr. Saunders, though that is not his name.

This little animal had had a hectic life from the very beginning. First of all, he was born during the hunting season, which would be unlucky for any baby squirrel. While he was still in the nest with his mother, a hunter came through the woods and, seeing no game, shot through the nest itself, one of the foulest and most contemptible acts any hunter can commit.

A wild animal, if shot while lying in its nest or den, will usually remain quiet even though badly injured, bleeding, and in agony, but this shot struck the mother in a vital spot and killed her. In her death throes, she threshed about so violently that she threw herself from the tree to the ground, hurling the baby out with her. Both seemed dead when they reached the ground, but presently the little one opened his eyes and made feeble crawling motions. The hunter picked him up and carried him home along with the dead mother.

He was given to Mr. Saunders, who took him to his fourth-grade schoolroom, where he became the adored pet of three dozen boys and girls, and was named Chip-Chip.

Part of this baby's harassed life is a story somewhat garbled and a little obscure but, as I understand it, he was entrusted to neighbors when Mr. Saunders was away on vacation. While there, "he got out of his cage, and when they tried to catch him, he bit two of them."

If left alone, a squirrel will play for a while, then return to his cage of his own volition. However, if he is pursued, he will panic, lose his head completely, and become frantic with fear. It is usually the terror and pain of being seized and held which causes a squirrel to bite a handler, especially a baby squirrel, which usually doesn't bite at all.

The neighbors then summoned a police officer to aid in subduing the monster, and he, with the usual misinformation about rabies, said, "Why, this animal might have hydrophobia!" and took him away to be confined and observed for symptoms, though he had not been near another animal.

The danger of rabies (hydrophobia) is not to be minimized,

but rabies does *not* develop spontaneously, as so many people seem to believe. Evidently a large segment of our population has the idea that an animal may suddenly "go mad" and break out with rabies, much as people break out with measles or chicken pox.

Rabies is spread through the bite (saliva) of an animal which has become infected and rabid after being bitten by another infected animal.

People who know no more about rabies than the name often become quite hysterical over an animal bite, and perform deeds as wild and uncontrolled as those of the most rabid dog. Frequently, they rush out and shoot the animal without waiting to find out whether or not it is infected, and make matters worse by shooting it through the head, which prevents examination of the brain. But even this examination would be useless if the animal was killed so soon after being bitten that a rabid condition was not yet apparent.

Authorities tell us that any person bitten by a warm-blooded animal which has had the opportunity to become infected (as some of them have) should take immediate steps to prevent this always-fatal disease. The animal should be confined (usually twenty-one days) for observation, and a doctor, health officer, or veterinarian consulted. If the confined animal *does* have the disease, it will usually die within a week, and there is still ample time for vaccine to be administered.

Rabies vaccine was first developed in 1885, by Louis Pasteur, and though it saved countless lives, it sometimes caused paralysis as well, and was therefore regarded with dread and apprehension until very recently. Since 1950, however, Indiana has pointed with pride to the development by the Eli Lilly Company (Indianapolis) of duck embryo rabies vaccine, which is just as effective as the Pasteur-type of treatment, and which does *not* cause paralysis.

Chip-Chip was nearly six months old when he was confined

on suspicion of rabies, though he could scarcely be considered a likely candidate, as he had never been near another animal since his mother died. He was then claimed by the country conservation officer because he was being held illegally. Like many residents of the state, young Mr. Saunders had not known that a permit or license was necessary, and had never applied for one.

A wild animal thus seized by a conservation officer is usually transported to the nearest state game farm and released there. When Mr. Saunders told me about little Chip-Chip, however, I doubted that this pet would be able to care for himself, as he had been in captivity since he was only a few weeks old. And so I applied for his custody, partly out of concern for him, partly because I wanted to make further study of these little animals for the book I meant to write about them.

Through the wires of the telephone company, I followed the conservation officer around the county, to the courthouse, into the sheriff's office, out to the city park, and into the next county, but never did catch up with him. I therefore phoned the state conservation office in Indianapolis, explained the case, and received permission to own this squirrel—but that was only the beginning.

The local conservation officer would not release the animal to me without written orders from the state enforcement officers, who would not give an order without an order from the conservation heads, who apparently never gave orders to anyone without orders from each other. I made numerous phone calls and talked to numerous officials, but like the harassed Persian poet, "ever came out the same door wherein I went."

Weeks went by and I was still busy telephoning, saying, "Inasmuch as the director has given me permission to keep this squirrel, which I intend to use for educational purposes, *why* can't it be released to me?"

A young man with a voice that flowed like soothing syrup explained all over again that our conservation officer was reluctant to relinquish an animal without specific orders from the enforcement division, the captain of which was reluctant to issue an order without specific orders from his superior, who was likewise reluctant to issue an order without specific orders from his superior. . . .

"This is incredible!" I exclaimed. "It's fantastic! I really ought to stop writing about squirrels and write about politicians!"

There was a moment's silence. Then the young man asked softly, "There's a difference?"

I talked again to the conservation officer, who was awaiting his orders, and again to the enforcement officer who was awaiting *his* orders, and so on. Lee said, "Why don't you just forget the whole thing? You can't fight City Hall!"

I said, "I've heard that men can't. But, you know what? Women *can!*"

At last, one fine snowy day, the conservation officer arrived, a tall and handsome man in a uniform that would have done credit to a Mexican general, and uttered the long-awaited syllables of the magic incantation: "You may now have the squirrel!"

This officer was a veteran in conservation work, and out of his years of training and experience had come much fascinating knowledge and many hilariously funny stories. One, which he told me that day, had to do with a call he received about illegal fishing. Three teen-age boys had been observed along an isolated creek, attempting to electrocute fish with an old-fashioned wall telephone.

This is done by trailing a wire in the water, then turning the crank as we did when ringing grandma's telephone at the Old Home Place. The ringing discharges a current which will kill any fish present.

There didn't seem to be any fish present just then, but the boys went on trying, laughing and talking. Meanwhile, the officer and his deputy, some distance apart, were discussing the situation over a walkie-talkie.

"They're now at the bend of the creek," reported the deputy, "and will soon be in front of you."

The officer then stepped out of some concealing willows almost into the path of the three boys, all of whom were so intent upon their work that they did not even notice him. One boy was doing the ringing, and also summoning.

(*Ring, ring.*) "Hello, little catfish!" he'd say. "Come right on up, little catfish. We're waiting for you right here. (*Ring, ring.*) Hello, little catfish! Can you hear me down there? Swim right this way, don't be bashful. (*Ring, ring.*) Hello, little catfish. . . ."

Suddenly his gaze encountered a pair of shiny brown boots. He lifted his eyes and beheld The Law.

"*Good-by,* little catfish!" he gulped, and hurled the telephone into the stream.

The officer told me some very interesting things about his work, but did not give me the squirrel until later.

"I'll bring it tonight," he said. "This interview is just part of my investigation."

"*Investigation?*" I cried, staggered.

"Yes, I've talked with several people about you. Routine, of course."

I thought as I showed him out: *What* sort of qualifications must I possess, for heaven's sake? I wondered if they had given him a sheaf of questions to be filled out, all in the usual governmental gibberish.

Does the applicant, to the best of your knowledge and belief, merit acquiesence and/or compliance re: the aforementioned petition (*No. 72D-K 4 MLTR-160*)?

State whether, in your opinion, the applicant (*see above, Section II, Paragraph 3B*) *possesses such amplitude of cerebral percipience as to capably ascertain the difference between a black walnut* (Juglans nigra) *and a buckeye* (Aesculus glabra).

I do solemnly swear (or avow) that the preceding answers are of the utmost veracity, and tendered without coercion or mental reservation. . . .

Anyway, that night he brought Chip-Chip, and a sadder little animal I have never seen. He had been given kindly and affectionate care while in the custody of the officer, but there was about him a timid, bewildered, almost apologetic air—and with good reason. He had been shot from his nest, then transported to the hunter's home, to Mr. Saunders' home, to the schoolroom, to the family that was supposed to care for him, to the car of the police officer, to confinement in an animal hospital, to the conservation officer's home, and finally to me. We decided at once that he was far less sensitive than Mimi or Groany, as they would have died of shock and terror if they had been subjected to so many different quarters, vehicles, and handlers.

Chip-Chip was very tame, however, and loved to play. After one or two days, he skipped, hopped, bucked, leaped, cavorted in every way a squirrel can, and was clutching at our fingers. We could see even then that he was going to be an enthusiastic hand-holder.

We put him in Mimi's old cage and were delighted to have a furry little pet again. Legally he was mine (I signed the papers and paid for a license) and I thought him cute and very dear, but my heart ached every time I looked at him, for he was not *my* little pet, or even an image of him. I had believed that if I ever had another squirrel, I would not miss Groany so much, but instead of easing my loss, Chip-Chip magnified it. How many people, I wondered, have learned this sad lesson after seeking out and marrying someone they thought might console them for the loss of a beloved wife or husband?

Chip-Chip did not resemble our other pets in the least, except that he, too, was a squirrel. He looked like Bushy, and he *was* like Bushy, in size, appearance, and personality; he was just as friendly, just as gregarious. Instead of turning his back upon our callers (as Mimi and Groany had done) he *loved* callers, would romp and play and hold hands with any who were interested. He seemed far less tense than the others, not easily alarmed, and I felt certain that going to the animal hospital in an improvised "sausage sack" would not bother him at all.

It was obvious, even to our untrained eyes, that he belonged to a different strain. In appearance, he was longer, slimmer, browner, smaller in build, less elegant, and less temperamental. His busy little hands were tinier than the hands of either Groany or Mimi; his hair was not as smooth or as fine. His tongue was moist (not dust-dry, as theirs had been), and when he washed his face, he first licked his hands as a kitten does, though he also brought moisture from his nose with a sniffing sound. He was by no means as neat as my meticulous little Groany, but his lick-and-promise grooming standards were superior to those of Mimi. He seemed to have less interest in gnawing, ate fewer fruits and succulent vegetables, and drank more water.

Soon after he became acquainted with us, Chip-Chip chose to belong to Jamie, and he is now considered *her* squirrel, not mine. He is very affectionate toward Lee and also toward me, "talks" to us eagerly, and sometimes comes running to hug my ankle with his furry little arms as Groany used to do. But he adores Jamie, listens for her step on the stairs in the mornings, and greets her with reaching arms as Mimi used to greet Lee.

Chip-Chip is quite a gabby little squirrel, and goes about uttering *mm . . . mm . . . mm*'s of one kind or another all day long, plays merrily until he is tired, then rests on any flat and convenient surface, meanwhile holding hands with whoever happens to be nearby. Jamie announced one day that she had discovered a dimple in his right cheek, which I thought quite as absurd as any statement Mr. Dubbs ever made, but later when I looked where she told me to look, I *did* see a dimple in his right cheek.

When word got around that we had a little squirrel so tame and friendly he would talk to you, hug your arm, and hold your hand, we were deluged with callers. So many people came to see him (and came back again, bringing friends) that my days were harassed and my schedules shattered. Despite my honest desire to share our fascinating little pet with them, I found myself thinking, with a new understanding, of something Bill once said to me.

"Friends is nice," he told me. "Friends is one of the greatest things in the world. I just don't know what we'd do without friends. But the dang fools'll drive you crazy!"

By the time we had had Chip-Chip a year, he felt very much at home with us, ceased to look apologetic and sad. His fall colors came early, maple-leaf tinges of red inside his elbows, on his legs, and on his cheeks. (The cheeks of Mimi and Groany always turned red in the fall, looking as if they had been carelessly rouged.)

Of course, some of his ways remind us of them. He, too, buries nuts in all sorts of odd corners, likes to play in a paper bag, will steal sugar from the bowl, and makes "swearing" movements with his lips when angry. One of his favorite games is leaping upon the edge of the wastebasket, riding on it while it tilts to one side, then leaping clear before it falls on him.

Like the other squirrels, he is full of curiosity, is a born explorer, and loves to rummage in cupboards. If, in some Never-Never Land, a decorator is ever called upon to furnish a room for a pet squirrel, it should contain:

1. A comfortable people-bed in which to hide, nap, and perhaps play games. (Mimi loved to skip, hop, and prance around *under* the bedspread on chilly days.)
2. A folding ladder for climbing up and down, with a top step wide enough for a resting shelf.

3. A clothesbasket filled with terry towels where one may sleep in comfort, or bury nuts in privacy.

4. A window through which to watch sunsets, or insult bluejays and other unwelcome visitors.

5. A TV to watch, and a radio which offers "favorite recordings."

6. A cupboard to explore, preferably stacked with linens under which to hide.

7. A table of goodies and a drawer of gadgets to steal.

8. A little rug on which to play. (Mimi had a little crocheted rug of her own; she skipped and hopped on it, rolled and tumbled with it in her arms. Groany liked to play on a shag rug, and so does Chip-Chip.)

Chip-Chip has a sharp little temper and often flies into small harmless rages, but never offers to charge or bite anyone. When angry, he barks or chatters, meanwhile jerking his tail around and round. His whiskers bristle, his nose twitches, he makes short and threatening lunges with his front feet, at the same time stamping his back feet, but these tantrums are only sound and fury signifying nothing.

Like all other squirrels, he has chosen a favorite eating place —Lee's left knee. We give him his breakfast when we sit down to our own, and he promptly selects some tidbit from his plate (a grape, a nut, or a piece of apple), takes it in his mouth, and comes scampering into the breakfast room. He then jumps upon Lee's left knee, with an air of one who feels himself entirely welcome, and eats his little bite contentedly. When Lee is away at mealtime, Chip-Chip will substitute my left knee, or Jamie's, as a dining couch. He would share all our meals in this way if allowed to do so.

One day he had a strawberry and several sunflower seeds on his plate (a thin metal ashtray), both favorite foods. He ate the strawberry first and left the seeds until later, but they stuck fast in a residue of strawberry juice. After several futile efforts to pull them out, he picked up the plate and carried it to

Jamie, an act very interesting to watch. First he stood up on his hind feet, as tall and straight as possible, with the little plate in his teeth. He then threw back his head and opened his jaws wide enough for it to fall back into the corners of his mouth, where he could get a good grip on it. After that, he scampered to Jamie without as much as tilting the plate, and leaped upon her lap, holding it out to her as though to say, "Please fix it. I don't know what to do."

He has learned to go to the sink to "ask" for water, which he drinks from a glass, and to the refrigerator for two of his favorite "treats": apples and ice cubes. Once he tasted some unsweetened tea left in a cup, and has been begging and drinking it ever since, about a spoonful at a time.

Apparently someone has fed him canned fruit, for he shows a great fondness for it, will "talk" eagerly and hopefully whenever he smells or sees it. Jamie often gives him pieces of peach or pear out of canned fruit cocktail, and these tiny cubes are just right for a small squirrel to handle. He also has an appetite for butter, and for wheat-germ oil which he will lick from Jamie's finger, or from a little plastic spoon. (Some naturalists recommend vitamins for pet squirrels, but we abandoned this plan because our pets were overstimulated by every type of vitamins we tried, becoming wildly restless and disturbed. For some reason, however, the outside squirrels did not appear to have the same reaction.)

Neither Mimi nor Groany would touch eggs, but Chip-Chip loves them. While he prefers a bit of egg that has been cooked and chopped, he will eat raw egg yolk just as readily, and doesn't care that it is messy. Jamie is always washing his face, but he doesn't seem to mind, and appears to think it a game played by climbing a washcloth.

Sometimes she plays with him by letting him climb a bath towel, which he does with the hand-over-hand ease of an old salt ascending a rope. And a good thing, too, for one day he leaped from her shoulder to the top of the refrigerator-freezer, and fell down behind it. Lee was gone, and Jamie and I could not move it, but she rescued him by lowering a bath towel, twisted in rope fashion, and he promptly climbed out.

Often he runs to Jamie and "asks" her to pick him up because he wants to be hoisted as though by a crane. She reaches down to him, and he holds tight to her hand, either by putting his arms around her wrist, or by gripping her forefinger with both little hands. He "grins" with glee as she lifts him up and swings him in the air.

He is extremely affectionate, loves to be petted, cuddled, and hugged. When he first came to us, Jamie would often pick him up and kiss the top of his head. Evidently he came to regard this as a very pleasing gesture of affection, for now he will go to all three of us in turn, presenting his head for this caress. Sometimes he will leap into Lee's lap and turn over on his back in the bend of Lee's arm, wanting to be cradled there for a while. Later, this same idea is suggested to Jamie, and to me.

When he was a baby, he was kept in a box, which probably explains why he never learned to like a sleeping bowl. After he had spent several restless nights, Lee built a box bed for him and put it on the shelf inside the cage. He rested peacefully and comfortably thereafter, tucked into terry blankets.

At night, if he hears one of us approaching through the darkness, he is instantly awake, and gives the low and ominous warning, "*Tut-tut-tut-tut-tut-tut!*" as though to say, "I'm right here, and wide awake, so just don't try anything!" If we come closer and touch him or speak to him, he is immediately reassured and goes back to sleep. No doubt squirrels in the woods use the same sounds to warn intruders coming near their dens at night.

Chip-Chip is probably no gabbier than were our other pets, but seems so because his voice is easier for us to hear. One day, much to Jamie's surprise I think, she heard him make the high, thin sound, almost like a scream, which I insisted that I had heard from Groany and Mimi. I was delighted to know that I had *not* imagined it, and that she too interpreted it as a demand for attention.

Chip-Chip is intelligent and perceptive in a way that reminds me poignantly of Shad. He, too, wanted to explore the linen cupboard in the back hall. It has a latch but not a lock, and to keep the squirrels from opening it, I slipped a yardstick through the curved door-pulls. Groany had always accepted defeat when this yardstick was in place, but not Chip-Chip! Somehow or other, he has managed to figure out that the yardstick is the reason he cannot open the cupboard. On cleaning days, when I have a ladder in the back hall, he will climb it as far as is necessary, then seize the end of the yardstick in his teeth and try to remove it by gnawing it and pulling at it.

He has also discovered that there is something about a knob which causes a door to open. When he wants to open the door in the den, he climbs up on a leather chair nearby, to bite and push and struggle with the knob.

Not only has he learned to open every cupboard in the kitchen, but he knows where his favorite foods are kept. He will fasten his teeth to the lower edge of a certain door, open it, reach in, and steal a piece of garlic. If we did not keep a watchful eye on him, he would reek of garlic most of the time.

The intelligence of the fox squirrel is not appreciated by everyone, but certainly by Mr. B. L. Peak, a patrolman in Dayton, Ohio. Last October he watched two squirrels scamper out to the highway carrying walnuts in their mouths, and leave them in the road for cars to crush.

"Then they'd dart out when all was clear and get the goodies," he reported.

Doubting his own eyes, perhaps, he went back several times to watch the squirrels, and each time found them busy with this ingenious form of nut-cracking. An account of his observations was published in the Dayton *Daily News*, and probably doubted by many readers who were not aware of a squirrel's intelligence and resourcefulness—but not by *us!*

All four of our pets, Shad, Mimi, Groany, and Chip-Chip, belonged to the family of Eastern fox squirrels. My friend Gertrude Ward, a biology professor, explained to me that the word *Eastern* refers to the range of this little animal in the United States. The range covers the entire eastern half of the country (with the exception of the extreme northeastern states) and reaches from the Canadian border and the Great Lakes, south to Florida and the Gulf Coast.

The word *fox*, she told me, relates to their color, which, generally speaking, is not unlike that of the red fox; *squirrel* is from the old French *esquireul*.

However, fox squirrels vary greatly, and though our first pets were of the same litter, they bore little resemblance to one another in either temperament or color. But Chip-Chip could have been Bushy's twin, and is as loving and gentle toward Jamie as Bushy was loving and gentle toward Vera. Not long ago I had a note from her:

Every time I clean a remote corner, sort some magazines, or search through a box of clippings on my desk, I turn up a memory —a small nut carefully buried, his favorite toy tucked away in a favorite hiding place. I can't even think of his loving ways without crying a little. One of my friends gave me some kittens to fill this lonely place in my life, and they are really precious, but I'd gladly trade them for one little you-know-what.

Today I read that the hunting season has started. It saddens and angers me to think that for $1.50, any moron can carry a gun into the woods, even when he doesn't know how to use it properly, and be allowed to maim, cripple, kill, or cruelly wound a squirrel. But one who would make a study of these little animals, do anything for their health, comfort, and welfare, must pay $5.00 a year, besides all the rigamarole you had to go through in the matter of red tape, applications, appeals, arguments, long-distance expenses, and monthly reports. . . .

Had not Bushy died with the same symptoms, we might have thought that Mimi had a communicable disease and infected Groany, but Bushy never saw either of them. They were all beautiful little animals, plump and lively and apparently healthy, with shiny coats and bright eyes, full of vigorous play. We had always made certain that they had fresh air, exercise, and foods that were natural to them. The cause of their death was a mystery, and my correspondence with authorities did not help me to solve it.

From a famous museum of natural history: "Tree squirrels, including the fox squirrel, are not difficult to keep in captivity. They feed upon a variety of foods, and I suggest simply trying various foods until you see what the animal will eat." (Trying "various foods" once sent little Groany into convulsions.)

From a noted curator of small mammals: "The gray squirrel has been known to live to an age of nine years. It is quite likely that fox squirrels may have a similar longevity."

From a university professor: "Squirrels that are free of mange and fleas will remain healthy indefinitely, with adequate quarters and food."

From the director of a university museum of natural history: "I am convinced that squirrels in the wild live less than a year."

From the Ohio Division of Wildlife: "We have had some experience rearing baby gray and fox squirrels . . . however, never with very much success. Our best longevity records on squirrels in the wild are: Three and a half years by a male fox squirrel, two and three-quarters years by a female gray squirrel." (Robert Donohoe)

In our own opinion, one of the best informed men in the field is *Karl Maslowski, noted Cincinnati naturalist,* to whom we turned several times for counsel, finding his suggestions thoughtful and wise, his conclusions accurate. He now wrote me: "I feel that you did very well with them, keeping them alive and in good health for more than five years. I am sure that in the wild very, very few squirrels ever reach that age."

His words were comforting to us, and to Vera, for now we know we did all that anyone could have done for these little childlike creatures who were so close to our hearts.